My Path to Spontaneous Healing

An Intuitive Woman's Extraordinary Experiences
Take You Beyond This Realm
to Healing and Inner Peace

Ms. Saulenas shows us how an ordinary life can be easily filled with remarkable experiences and amazing healing.

Sharon Saulenas

Published by BookLocker.com, Inc., Trenton, Georgia, U.S.A.

Printed on acid-free paper.

BookLocker.com, Inc.
2022

DISCLAIMER

This book details the author's personal experiences with and opinions about spontaneous healing, death and dying, life after death, and the health and well-being benefits of developing Intuition and living in the moment. The author is not a healthcare provider.

The author and publisher are providing this book and its contents on an "as is" basis and make no representations or warranties of any kind with respect to this book or its contents. The author and publisher disclaim all such representations and warranties, including for example warranties of merchantability and healthcare for a particular purpose. In addition, the author and publisher do not represent or warrant that the information accessible via this book is accurate, complete or current.

The statements made about products and services have not been evaluated by the U.S. Food and Drug Administration. They are not intended to diagnose, treat, cure, or prevent any condition or disease. Please consult with your own physician or healthcare specialist regarding the suggestions and recommendations made in this book.

Except as specifically stated in this book, neither the author or publisher, nor any authors, contributors, or other representatives will be liable for damages arising out of or in connection with the use of this book. This is a comprehensive limitation of liability that applies to all damages of any kind, including (without limitation) compensatory; direct, indirect or consequential damages; loss of data, income or profit; loss of or damage to property and claims of third parties.

You understand that this book is not intended as a substitute for consultation with a licensed healthcare practitioner, such as your physician. Before you begin any healthcare program, or change your lifestyle in any way, you will consult your physician or other licensed healthcare practitioner to ensure that you are in good health and that the examples contained in this book will not harm you.

This book provides content related to topics physical and/or mental health issues. As such, use of this book implies your acceptance of this disclaimer.

To my sister, Rosemarie Forgione
with loving gratitude

A beautiful, bright shining star
who lit up my life and lifted me
~ simply by being herself.

Contents

A Note to the Reader

Thank you for choosing to read this book.

My hope is that it will inspire you to begin to live your life from that place of knowing that anything is possible and that you, I, and everyone are One. *No one* is excluded. No one is disconnected ...even if it may sometimes feel that way.

By sharing what I've learned and experienced I'm going to show you what's possible and how each of us has the ability to bring healing, peace, and happiness into our lives.

We are living at a very exciting time! The energy around the planet is said to be rising very rapidly. This affects all who are on it. Each day more and more of us are opening to new gifts, and having experiences and abilities beyond our known senses. This is happening at all different ages, all around the globe. If you did not experience any of this in your childhood or even in your life up to now, please know that it can still happen at any time.

Even as many are caught up in anger, drama and chaos, many wonderful things are happening in the world as well. This is a very opportune time to begin a practice of self-awareness and inward exploring.

To get the most benefit from this book, I suggest you read it through a second time as different pieces will stand out for you at different times. When you are in doubt or are feeling alone on your path, it will be here to lift you. It will remind you of the unlimited possibilities available to you when you pause, return to the present moment, and practice connecting to your Inner Wisdom, your Divine Self.

It is my wish that the experiences I share with you will show you the way to inner peace and a renewed sense of purpose. They take the mystery out of why something may feel missing in your life and offer hope, direction, and love. Yes, love... because I have infused each of them with it as I wrote them out for you.

Enjoy!

Introduction

Before I share some of my experiences, I would like to tell you how I became known to a very loving, but puzzled friend as "The Girl With Too Many 'Haps'".

I have been very blessed in my life. Generally, I love life more and more with each passing year. There is so much to each season of our lives it seems we almost need separate lifetimes to experience each changing age!

I have always believed in Divine Miracles, Goodness and Love. That might sound cliche'd to some of you, however, my life has been filled with these wonderful things.

That is not to say that I am blind to suffering and the many painful challenges that we often face. Like so many of us, I have personally struggled through great hardship and times when I fell out of trust and into fear; times when I felt smothered by heartbreak or fear and temporarily gave up hope rather than connecting with, and trusting in my 'Inner Wisdom', our Divine Source, for guidance.

I have known the deep pain and heart wrenching-sorrow of a spouse's passing. I have been told by a number of specialists that I would never fully recover from severe, debilitating injuries. I have lost my income and my home and lived in poverty. For a period of time, I was terrorized in the night as a young child (I felt there was no hope for

1

escape. The threat to harm my little brother if I told loomed over me), and much, much more.......... I would often find myself running from my situation or trying to fix it, rather than going inside to find solace and guidance from my Divine core.

The pain and terrible sorrow arrived when I resisted change and insisted on how my life or circumstances *should* be, or how others *should* be rather than accepting the situation laid out for me and following my Inner Wisdom, the Higher Love that lives in us all, the Divine Love that we are. These were times when I felt trapped or smothered and temporarily gave up hope, rather than connecting with Divine Love and feeling that love and inner comfort as I moved through a terrible situation.

Always, whenever I finally stopped and came back to being fully present in the moment and returned to trusting and connecting with my Inner Wisdom, I was brought out of fear and back to inner peace. That practice of living in the moment, noticing the signs around me, going inside and connecting with the Divine force, the Supreme love that guides and connects us all, brought me through.

We all know that some fears are easier to overcome than others. Some can take time. Most often we are so caught up in the drama of life around us that we do not even recognize our own fears. All too often we deliberately hook into the drama so we don't have to face the fears. We run from them by looking around and deciding that it is someone or something outside of ourselves that is creating our unhappiness rather than realizing it is our own fear holding us back from the joy that is <u>always</u> there waiting for us to recognize and embrace it.

Some of us have been raised to believe that all of this is hogwash but it's 100% true in my experience.

I believe trust is both a process and a practice. There is so much fear around us that it is easy to be swept in and swallowed up by it. Each day, in every moment and every situation, you and I have a choice. We can choose happiness, love, and fun, or we can be unhappy, unloving and distressed or apathetic. I can't tell you that I always choose the former, but much of my time, I do. So much so, that this dear friend shared a theory about it. He came upon this theory a while ago, and inspired by my generally joyful nature, felt he should share it with me:

So it goes that we all come into this world with a certain number of 'haps' (a hap being a unit of measure, specifically, a unit of happiness). Based on his observations and experiences, it seems to him that everyone is not allotted the same number of haps, and that I received far more than average. This, he believes, is the explanation for my continued delight in life, despite the major life-changing challenges I have faced at times.

I think it's a very entertaining theory! It makes me smile and sometimes laugh when I consider it. I love him. Yet he continues to be so utterly perplexed by my lifelong joy. He tells me it simply isn't humanly possible to be happy so much of the time.

However, since I am human, and I do derive great joy and delight from this ever-changing adventure we call life, it seems he's mistaken.

My version of his 'hap' theory would be more like this: 'Haps' are more like bulbs on a hypothetical string of beautiful holiday lights that are given to us all, some of which may just be loose or covered. They are not broken or defective, but they sometimes need to be adjusted, one by one, to clear the connection that will make them shine. Unfortunately, most of us don't know how to do that or that we even *can* do that, so often they remain unlit.

This is why I believe in building a practice that is part of our daily routine, one that causes us to pause, go inside, and connect with our Inner Wisdom, the Source that lights those 'bulbs', the Divine Love that lives in us all, because it is truly there. And the great thing is, we all have access to it.

For those of you that are unsure, reaching out to someone who can guide you there and teach you how to connect with your Divine Source, or point you back when you slip off into the drama of life, is crucial.

I imagine that my shining 'haps' come from my deep belief

in, and connection with, our Divine Source. The connection comes from staying present and living in the moment. I believe that a 'hap' is an expression of gratitude and love, and that happiness is our true nature; it lives inside each of us. All it takes is the desire and focus to access it.

But that's a story for another time.

Today I want to share a few pieces of my life with you. Simple pieces. Intimate pieces. Pieces that are part of a string of events that began early in my childhood.

I share them with you to give you a glimpse into greater possibilities.

I share them in the hope that they inspire you to create or maintain that practice of going inside and listening to your inner voice, to notice the signs around you, to live in the moment and connect with the Divine Higher Love that guides and connects us all.

I also share them for those of you that have already been given the gift of a 'sixth sense', such as heightened intuition, mediumship, extended sight, etc.

Please know that you are ok and you are not alone.

And for the times when your Light seems dim or feels blocked for a while, know that I am here doing my best to shine Light out to you,

~ Always wishing you well.

Learning to Trust

My great aunt's house and her large expanse of yard was across the narrow dirt lane from my family's home, and my grandparent's house was a short 2-minute walk down the same lane. There were no other houses close by until a neighborhood was built down the street when I was 14. Before that, it was only our homes surrounded by acres and acres of woods, a swamp, and a couple of meadows. There was a small pig farm tucked back into one part of the woods as well. So, until I was in the first grade, my playmates were my brother Steve and some of our cousins when they came visiting every day during the summer and on weekends during the school year.

I grew up spending time each day in nature and with our many animals. Exploring and climbing trees, watching the squirrels and the birds, rolling around in the tall grass and flowers of a sun-filled meadow, and skating on the ponds in the winter were all natural parts of my early days. At 10, our neighbor at the pig farm invited me to ride his pinto pony. He had gotten the pony for his son who wanted nothing to do with it. He said he needed someone to exercise it and a whole new world opened for me when I easily learned to ride western style. I immediately fell in love with 'Pepper' and rode and cared for him nearly every day. We became so in tune to one another that it felt as though we were one as we would race at full speed from one end of the meadow to the other. It felt like we were flying!

At home, we always had dogs, sometimes cats, my pet goat, chickens, and later 'Thunder' our Shetland pony and 'Poncho' my grandfather's sweet horse. Our animals were like part of the family.

I felt very connected to our Divine Source, to my family, and to nature. The trees and animals were often my outdoor companions. Spending time in nature, with animals, and with kind, happy people allowed my Intuition(Inner Wisdom) to develop. I would often 'know' things or be given 'messages' through feelings in my body and/or a sudden 'knowing' that came into my awareness.

So, it was very distressful for me at 18, to begin getting these sudden 'messages' that someone was about to die! I could not understand why our Divine Source was showing me this as I could do nothing to prevent it.

The messages began with Sammy. Sammy was a quiet boy who sometimes hung around with my brother Steve. He was a nice kid who I often saw when I was walking, biking, or now driving in the area where he lived. Each time I saw him, which was almost daily, I would wave and he would wave back.

One day I was shaken to my core! I was driving out of a store parking lot and saw him across the street. We waved our usual greeting to each other. Suddenly, a message flashed into my head like a news bulletin! It was bold and clear and told me that Sammy was about to die. I was horrified! I tried to shake it off but it stayed with me for a while that day. The next day I learned that Sammy had been attempting to cross the highway mere hours after I had seen him and been hit by a car. He had died instantly. It was terrible news!

Weeks later I met up with a few friends from high school. We were catching up on how everyone was enjoying the summer. We began mentioning other classmates we had run into and reported on how they were doing as well. It was a nice beginning to our new life as graduates. When someone mentioned our classmate Holly and how great she was doing, another 'bulletin' instantly flashed into my head informing me that she was about to die very soon! Again, I was shocked and horrified, but at that time I just couldn't share what was happening to me. I couldn't begin to explain it since I couldn't really understand it myself!

The following day I learned the heart-wrenching news that this bright, vibrant girl with an exciting future was killed later the same evening that I had met with my friends! She had a terrible accident while driving home from visiting a friend. We were all devastated.

Later, that very same summer, I was walking along the road to meet a friend. Another friend's younger brother Billy came cycling by on the other side, heading in the opposite direction. He stopped for a few minutes and we chatted and laughed across the empty street. As we said goodbye and he began to pedal away, the dreaded 'message' came storming into my head again. It just couldn't be true! It was such a beautiful, bright, sunny summer day. The temperature was perfect, and we were both so happy and carefree. I just couldn't imagine him dying that day. It just didn't seem possible! Hours later, however, the entire neighborhood and beyond would be horribly shocked and numbed for weeks. We were all absolutely dumbstruck by the tragic news we received.

It turned out that when Billy had stopped to chat with me, he had been on his way to meet up with some friends in the woods nearby. While they were waiting for other friends to arrive, he had decided to climb one of the high-tension electrical towers that ran through that part of the woods to see if he could see them coming. He assured his friends that he wasn't going to climb anywhere close to the wires. However, unbeknownst to him and the others watching him climb, there was a deadly arc of electricity that could easily reach him, even though he never got nearly close enough to touch the wires. Once struck, he fell several feet to the ground below. It happened so quickly and unexpectedly that his friends were momentarily frozen in time as they attempted to comprehend the morbid sight. Then, screaming in horror, they ran for help. It was a terribly gruesome event that marked their young lives forever... another message of death that came to pass.

There were others. I prayed and prayed and asked for guidance. At some point I finally surrendered and trusted that there was a Higher purpose at work here. Soon after, those particular messages stopped.

Later, as a nurse caring for hospitalized patients, I could often walk into a room and suddenly 'know' that something had shifted with my patient's condition. One time I even sensed one of my trauma patients becoming septic. (Sepsis is a potentially life-threatening condition caused by the body's response to severe infection.) Even though he was without complaint, in no noticeable distress, and his vital signs were still stable, I immediately called the resident for orders. Of course, he asked for vital signs. I told him they were still normal but I knew that they were about to change. He didn't really understand but he trusted me and gave standing orders to use 'if' the patient began to show signs. I then went back in the room, took another set of vital signs, and saw they were now changed. I was able to draw the necessary blood work at once and it later confirmed what I had reported. With early treatment the patient quickly recovered.

There was also the time my eighty four year old mother was in ICU recovering nicely from emergency abdominal surgery. When I walked in, she was resting comfortably and was glad to see me. Suddenly, just standing beside her bed, I could clearly 'hear' fluid collecting inside her lungs! I called for her nurse and told him that she had some fluid in her lungs and asked if she was getting medication to remove it. "Oh, no" he said. "I just listened to her lungs about 15 minutes ago and they were clear." So I asked if he would give them another quick listen, which he did. He was surprised to confirm what I had told him and treated her at once. Her grateful lungs responded nicely.

As a Hospice nurse working with dying patients, most often I would 'know' or sense when it was their time to pass on. These were much softer, gentler 'knowings' rather than the harsh blaring 'bulletins' from earlier times.

A Stroke of Insight

When I decided to become a registered nurse, I felt it would be a good stepping stone while I was contemplating what to truly do with my life. I never expected to love it so completely. It suited me well. I love people and I've always derived joy from helping others feel better. The workings of the body fascinate me and I've always been interested in healing and assisting others with their end-of-life needs and concerns. My strong intuitive sense has always helped me with every aspect of this.

I believe a number of nurses have a highly developed intuition, or 'sixth sense', where they can tell what is going on with their patient even when they cannot see it. This was one of those many times for me:

I was still a student nurse when my grandmother fell ill. One day after school, I received a terribly distressing call from my mother. Blurting out the words, she anxiously told me that my grandmother (her mother) was not responding at all. She rushed on to say that the doctor had told her that my grandmother had suffered a stroke!

At this I felt my gut clench and my breath catch in my throat. After a few moments I realized I needed to calm myself. So I took some deep breaths, asked for Divine guidance and hurried over to see my grandmother.

When I arrived, she was lying in bed like a mannequin. Her eyes were open and when I looked into them, I immediately 'knew' that she hadn't had a stroke. Throughout my life I have experienced this sudden sense of 'knowing' that leads me to a Truth. Something else was going on. When I asked her if she could squeeze my hand, her fingers stirred slightly on only one hand in acknowledgement. I heard my mother gasp in horror as I told my grandmother that she did not have a stroke. I told her that I knew it was something else and would get to the bottom of it.

I softly said "I know this must be very scary for you, but just try to rest while I figure this out, ok?"

My grandmother and I had a very close relationship and I knew she trusted me. Once again, her fingers barely fluttered in acknowledgement. I then got up and went over to my mother who quickly ushered me out of the room, anxiously asking why I had given my grandmother false hope by telling her that she hadn't had a stroke when clearly, she had. I told her the doctor was mistaken, that she did not have a stroke.

"How can you say that!", she cried, objecting loudly.

"Because I just 'know' she didn't," I replied.

At that she demanded to know how I could be so sure. Again, all I could tell her was that I just 'knew.'

As you might imagine, she wasn't very happy with me but she was also horrified at the thought of her mother having had such a terrible injury to her brain and body. After all, she still carried the awful memory of having witnessed her own beloved grandmother, (her mother's mother) suffer a massive stroke so many years earlier. I asked her about any new medications because I had a very strong feeling that it was related and she told me that there were none. I asked her to go over the medications with me again. Although she couldn't sit still and was irritated and frightened, she complied. She said, "There were only three." I asked her at what times they were given and if anything was given with them, anything at all. After asking the question a few times, a few different ways, despite her annoyance with me, she suddenly remembered that the doctor had recommended that my grandmother also start taking a mild tranquilizer twice a day. She went on to assure me that she had been given only one dose and that was over an hour earlier. She said it was a very low dose, actually the very lowest one. She went on to tell me that she herself had taken this same medication before at this dose and it hadn't bothered her at all. She was certain it did not affect my grandmother so dramatically as this.

Although this was not a known response to this medication, as soon as she mentioned the drug, I immediately 'knew' without a doubt that it was the culprit! My inner voice had been telling me that the problem was medication related but it didn't jibe with what my mother had originally reported to me. Now I knew for certain that this was the result of the medication, regardless of the very small dose. I was thrilled!

"That's it!" I told her. "She's going to be fine!"

To my mother's renewed horror, I turned and hurried back in to my grandmother's room. I leaned close to her again and softly told her that we had figured it out, that it was the medication, the new pill she had taken a while ago that caused her to be like this. I told her again that I could only imagine how terribly frightening it must be to feel like this and not know what happened. I assured her that the medication would soon wear off and asked if she could try to relax and rest until then. I also assured her that one of us would be nearby and would be checking in on her until she was better. Again, a few fingers trembled in acknowledgement. I could see the relief in her eyes.

I was able to help my grandmother by pausing to center myself, letting go of the fear, and opening to, and trusting in Divine guidance.

My mother and I loved my grandmother very much. We were both immensely relieved when she returned completely to normal after the medication wore off hours later.

Death With Dignity

After finishing my junior year in nursing school for my RN, I sat for and passed the LPN (Licensed Practical Nurse) state boards so I could work as a licensed nurse and use some of my skills while finishing school for my RN. During time off I took a position on the night shift in a medical unit. There was a night Charge Nurse, myself, and a CNA (Certified Nurse's Assistant) for 30-40 patients. More than half of them were elderly individuals that were at, or close to, their end-of-life time. Some were awake and responsive, others were not.

One of my duties was to go around with my CNA every two hours to turn and reposition our bedridden patients for comfort and to help prevent bedsores, etc. Each time, I would gently remind them of who we were, why we were there, what we were going to do, and why. I always assumed that all of my patients could hear and understand me, even if they were unresponsive. I was responsible for their care and comfort and I treated them as I would a member of my own family. In a sense, while at work, they were my extended family. We would carefully turn and reposition them, fix their hair, rub their back, etc., while spending a few moments letting them know that they were being cared for and were not alone.

Quite often one of our very ill elderly patients would die on our shift. When this happened, once the physician had pronounced them dead, we would lovingly perform their postmortem care which included respectfully administering to their physical body while making sure that their three means of identification were correct and in place. We would always cleanse them as needed, fix their hair, apply a fresh gown, and place their body in a dignified position. All of this we did with great care while honoring the essence of the person. It was also our chance to say goodbye.

Once the person was pronounced dead by the physician, it was also part of our duty to bring their body to the morgue, which generally occurred deep in the night. The difficulty with this was my assistant. Just the thought of going to the morgue terrified her. The hospital was old and the morgue was deep in the bowels of the building. The morgue itself was left in total darkness. Rolling the heavy, clumsy stretcher carrying the now lifeless body down the vacant halls, onto the creaky, empty elevator, we descended into the scary old basement alone. There was never another soul around.

Once there, we traveled the dim, eerily lit corridors to our gloomy destination. I would open the door to the morgue, feel around in the chilly darkness to find the light switch, and roll the stretcher in. Often, I had to place it beside another cold, grey body or two.

The room belonged to the dead.

It was like entering a freezer! It was small, cramped and filled with arctic air. There was hardly any room to manage the bulky stretcher. My thin uniform did little to prevent the deep chill from washing through me like an ice-cold wave.

The first time I went down to the morgue with my assistant, she refused to go in. No amount of convincing could get her to change her mind. She hated even going down into the creepy old basement. This meant that I had to maneuver the clumsy, antiquated stretcher through the doorway and into the morgue, placing it in the designated area by myself. An impossible task without banging it up against the doorframe going in, and once inside, against the other stretchers, which quietly held other still, lifeless bodies.

Now I do know that a deceased person is no longer in body. Still, it felt disrespectful to be banging their body, or the bodies of others, around like that. So, I spoke to my supervisor about it. She was sympathetic but told me there was no other help available. It just seemed like a terrible system so I decided to do what I could to improve it.

At home the next morning I sat quietly and asked for guidance. That next night I spoke to my CNA again and told her that if she could trust me, she would not have to make any more dreaded trips down into the creepy old basement in the middle of the night. She was a bit perplexed but interested and we went about our nightly routines as usual.

One night, as we entered a patient's room to reposition him, I suddenly 'knew' intuitively, as I usually did, that when we repositioned him this time, he would pass on. I shared this with my CNA and explained that I am often given 'messages' from the Divine by way of a sudden knowing that comes into my thoughts, and that they guide me in my life and my healing. I suggested the option of letting our patient sleep, and coming back to check on him to be sure he was comfortable. She had difficulty trusting this and worried about not turning him. I assured her that he would be passing only two hours later, at his first turn in the morning. Still, she could not trust, which I fully understood. I admired her dedication to her patient's care and did not press her. As we very gently turned our patient onto his side, he passed on. She was shocked.

A few nights later, close to morning, as we entered another unresponsive patient's room, I got the same 'message.' Again, I gave her a choice. She was hesitant but reluctantly agreed. We gently moved the pillows that held 'Elaina' propped on her side. This small movement just shifted her position slightly. Now she could sleep on undisturbed. We checked on her during the remaining two hours we had left to work, spending a few moments whispering reassuringly to her. Finally, our shift ended and she remained resting quietly. When we returned for work that night, we learned that she had passed on with the first turn of the morning. My CNA was astounded.

From then on, if one of our terminally ill patients had begun labored breathing, she would assume that we wouldn't be turning them. Most often I would tell her, "No, it's not his/her time yet" (no matter how bad they looked or sounded) and we would gently reposition them and spend a few moments before leaving to make sure they were still comfortable and that they knew we were always close by. However, each time I got 'the message' she was happy to let them rest comfortably, undisturbed. We would continue to tend to them. Each time, without fail, they rested easy and then passed on during the first turn on the day shift.

During the day, all the lights were all on in the basement, the morgue was open and lit, and there was adequate staff. Our daytime floor staff did not have to leave the unit to travel there. Caring, well trained help was available that was respectful and competent in the proper and dignified transporting of the newly departed. We both felt it was a more honorable and dignified way to treat our 'adopted family members.'

After a few months the day shift began to wonder why patients had stopped dying on our shift and why so many were dying first thing in the morning on thcirs - a puzzle they never solved!

This is not to say that I can predict the moment everyone is going to die. Just as often as I am given a 'message' as to when it will occur, at other times it is left unknown. Sometimes during these times, I 'get' that people are completing unfinished business on a deeper level. Other times it just feels like it is not meant to be known. Often this has to do with a person close to the dying person. I have seen individuals wait for people they love to leave the room. Other times I have seen those that are ready to transition hang on beyond what seems humanly possible and wait for certain people to arrive.

One heartwarming example of this is when my Aunt Dot died. She had very advanced illness and her frightfully diminished body barely made a bump in the bedcovers. The doctor finally suggested that they stop all treatment and allow her to pass peacefully.

My aunt was my mother's sister and my mother was at her side each day. Aunt Dot confided to her that more than anything she wanted to see her son Billy one last time. Sadly, Billy was serving a few months in jail as a first-time offender for a poor choice he had made. My mother was determined to get him out for a visit. She began contacting the jail daily as soon as she found out her sister was dying. Although they continually delayed their decision, she was persistent and each day she assured my aunt that Billy would be released for a visit. They were both hopeful but after a few weeks my aunt fell into a coma. My mother pleaded and appealed to the warden's sense of humanity. At the same time, she asked the doctor, who was aware of the situation, to put my aunt's IV back in with the hope that the hydration would help her hold on a little longer.

The doctor responded by saying, "It would be of little or no help. All of her internal organs are shutting down. She will pass at any time now."

"I don't care!" My mother replied. "I want her IV back in."

Reluctantly, he agreed. She just knew she was very close to getting Billy out for a visit.

Finally, it happened. Only a few weeks away from his scheduled release, the jail agreed to furlough him for a few hours under my mother and father's supervision. My mother was ecstatic! Each day she had been telling her sister that Billy would be there soon and now she could tell her that he would be there tomorrow!

Although my aunt was completely unresponsive, my mother trusted that she could still hear and understand her.

The following day my parents picked Billy up and brought him to see his mother. Before they went outside the room to give him some private time, Billy pulled a chair close to the bed. He took his mother's hand and said, "Mom, it's Billy. I'm here Mom."

Silence...... My aunt did not move, or squeeze his hand or even blink. As my parent's held their breath, suddenly, an enormous tear appeared in one of her eyes - the eye nearest her son. It swelled up and then tumbled forward, slowly rolling down her cheek. They all watched spellbound, realizing that she had heard him! She knew he was there! My parents were thrilled. Billy stayed by his mother's side until he had to go back. His mother passed peacefully shortly afterwards.

If we could know the time of everyone's death, imagine how different life would be. Some answer by saying they would treat the person better, show more love, spend more time with them... So why wait? Why not do that now?

In every moment, all around the globe, people die in many different ways, at all different ages. Death is meant to occur just as it does and when it does. Life and history tell us this over and over again. Some deaths are meant to be sudden and shocking, while others are peaceful or long and drawn out. With some, the cause remains unknown and yet others are so unique as to be completely beyond explanation. From my experience with those that have passed on, I believe we all agree on a higher level to the time of our passing and the way in which our death will occur.

If you believe we are all connected, as I do, you can understand that dying and death are very personal experiences, while at the same time everyone, especially those close to an individual, and even those that know or know of the person, are part of the death and dying on a deeper level.

Think about it. How has the death of a loved one, friend, acquaintance, or someone in the news, impacted your life?

~ More on this at another time...

Simple Repositioning

Shortly after becoming an RN, I moved from the Boston area to Houston, Texas with my friend P. We found a great, spacious apartment with our own walk-in closets, a private patio, and a huge swimming pool. Even as the hot, humid South Texas weather took some getting used to, we were having a great time enjoying the pool and the sunshine and exploring the lively city of Houston.

Within the Texas Medical Center, we both easily found jobs to our liking in different hospitals. Initially, P had regular daytime hours on an Oncology unit while I worked a 12-hour day shift alternating between a Trauma unit and an Adult Burn unit in another hospital. If we had a lot of emergencies on our unit, as we often did, my 12 hour shifts sometimes ran into 13 or 14 hours. Although being constantly on my feet was tiring at times, it was nice having the continuity of care with my patients. I also loved having three days off one week and four the next!

Returning to work each week after my days off, I looked forward to working with my 'second family'. I was proud to be a part of the nurses, ward clerks, residents and physicians that formed our elite team. The other nurses and I were specially trained and together we functioned as a cohesive, expert team that knew each other's strengths and weaknesses and performed smoothly as a unit because of it.

We supported each other and took the high-quality care we provided very seriously. We also had the good fortune of working with one of the best unit managers ever, and we all knew it. Althea was not only an amazingly capable manager, she was also a great nurse, a good person, and a fierce advocate for her patients and staff. She did whatever it took to keep us well-staffed, even occasionally taking patients herself during her time off, rather than leave us or our patients compromised by being short-staffed. She respected and supported us and under her guidance we became the best nurses we could be. We all felt the greatest admiration for her. For myself, it was an honor to be part of her team.

Although very demanding at times, we all enjoyed our work. Our patients did very well. Our infection rate was nearly non-existent and some of our patients came back to visit us months or even a year or more later to show us how well they were doing and to thank us again. Each week after time off, I was ready to rejoin my colleagues and devote my full attention to my patient's care and well-being.

One morning, after returning from 3 days off, I returned to work on the trauma unit. After changing into scrubs, I sat to listen to a detailed, updated report on my patients and a general report on the other patients on the unit as well. During this time, I heard screaming and cursing from a new teenage patient that had traumatically lost one of his legs a couple of days earlier when it had been instantly crushed in an accident. He was only 17.

The cursing and yelling continued as I checked in with my patients and did my initial assessments and treatments. When I finally managed a few free moments, I went to see what was going on. During report I had heard that this poor boy was very angry and difficult and was acting out a lot. His nurse was clearly distressed over his continued discomfort so I went and asked what he was so upset about. She told me that he kept asking her to move his foot - the one that wasn't there!

I asked if I could speak with him and she immediately agreed as she was happy to try anything to help him feel better. When I went in to see him, he was screaming and began hurling obscenities at me when he saw me. I stood there a moment, not even able to remotely imagine what he must be going through... to be seventeen and in an instant, have lost a leg. My heart went out to him. When he stopped for a moment, I calmly introduced myself and told him I had just come back from time off and didn't know what was going on with him but that I wanted to try to help. He was sitting up and began pounding his fists on the bed on either side of him. He started back hollering about needing help and that no one was helping him. At one point he grabbed his empty IV pole and slammed it down on the floor. Through a litany of shouts and curses he told me that his heel was killing him! He needed someone to move it, that it had been in the same position forever and no one would help him. I asked him which foot and he very angrily yelled "that one, stupid!" - pointing to his amputated leg. I took this opportunity to ask if I could move the sheet and take a look. He yelled "Ya!", while at the same time whipping the sheet off exposing the bandaged stump, and an empty area where his knee and lower leg should have been.

I very gently said "You do know this leg was amputated, right?" (I wanted to check his clarity)

He screamed, "YA, BUT IT'S KILLING ME!!! JUST MOVE IT!!! JUST F---ING MOVE IT!!!"

At this I looked down and 'saw' that the energetic form of his leg and foot was still there and intact. I told him that I would reposition it for him.

He angrily shouted "GOOD, JUST F---ING DO IT!"

I then slid my hands under his stump and the ever-present 'energy body' of his missing limb. This I 'saw' as something like an almost ghostly energetic shape of the physically missing part of his leg. I gently lifted it, supporting the stump and his 'ankle' and turned it slightly, repositioning it just as carefully and gently as I would a badly injured or painful physical leg. Then I gently set it back down on the bed in a slightly different position. He immediately let out a huge sigh of relief and an exasperated "FINALLY!"

I told him I was glad I could help. I straightened the sheet back over him, asked if he needed anything else (which he did not), picked up the IV pole, and told him I had to get back to my patients. I told him I was sorry he had to wait so long for relief and to let his nurse know if he needed my help again. He surprised me as I started out of the room by quietly saying "Thank you."

His nurse was shocked and delighted when the yelling stopped and wanted to know what I had done. I told her and suggested she try it. She was unable, however, to view or perceive his energy body so I planned to go back to see him as soon as I had a short break and show him how to move his 'foot' himself, hoping he would be receptive. Once I reached a point in the day where I had a few moments to spare, I went back. I imagined that he was a good kid, just shocked, angry and frightened - understandably so.

I found him to be very bright and glad to learn how he could help himself in this way.

The energy body remains even when part of the physical body is removed. My experience has been that if you regularly keep part of your focus there and continue to accept it as part of your being, you can have a much fuller experience with the missing limb or digit. This is most notable when people are given advanced prosthetics to wear and they become like a fully functioning second arm/leg, etc. to them.

My choice to stay present with this teen and not get caught up in his anger allowed me to be fully receptive and 'see' and feel his leg as it had existed prior to the accident. My willingness to honor what he was feeling brought great comfort to this terribly traumatized young man. For myself, any comfort or joy I can help bring to another makes my heart shine.

He remained stable, and was transferred to another unit two days later to eventually prepare for rehab. Word came through later that he had done very well!

A Bit About Miracles

As I said earlier, I have always believed in Divine miracles and I experience them regularly, both large and small.

We all do. It's simply a matter of staying present and paying attention.

The popular saying, 'Expect a Miracle' is so true because they are constantly occurring all around us each day. Some are very dramatic, like suddenly being completely healed of multiple injuries. Others are so small we often take them for granted... like when you misplace your keys and then find them just in time to arrive on time; or when you pull out into a roadway and suddenly another car comes speeding out of nowhere and narrowly misses you... you know it could have just as easily hit you. Even taking a breath in and out with ease, one after the other is a miracle!

As a nurse I have known so many people that have struggled exhaustively for each breath they took. They would expend all of their energy struggling to take one breath after another. It's a truly terrible thing. So imagine what a miracle it is to those of us that have no difficulty taking those breaths without even having to consciously think about it! Perhaps the saying should be 'Notice the Miracles!"

In my experience, the more one notices them, the more joy-filled and magical life begins to feel. I also believe that the more you notice, and the more gratitude you feel, the more healing takes place on many levels...so pay attention. Find people and things to feel grateful for. Staying in the present moment and noticing these 'gifts from the Divine', either large or small, further solidifies our feeling of connection to our Divine Source. The more present we are, the more we can feel love and experience joy and inner peace. That is the most healing of all!

Love in a Coma

Papa John was a transfer from another hospital. He was in a coma and dying when he arrived on our unit. (This was one of those brief, rare times that we had some unfilled trauma beds and would accept short-term patients.)

Word was that he had suffered severe, multiple organ damage from several failed surgeries and widespread infection at another hospital. This had left him in a coma, completely unresponsive. His prognosis was extremely poor.

He was a striking man of 60 who looked far younger than his age. With his imposing build, thick shock of pure white hair and electric ice blue eyes, he looked as if he truly could have been a Viking.

His care included, among other things, tending to the many wounds and various drains coming from multiple areas of his torso, as well as frequent suctioning of his airway where loose mucous would regularly collect. Papa John was unable to even clear his own throat so suctioning was necessary. It involved having a narrow, single-use suction catheter inserted in one nostril and passed down to the back of his throat to clear it for him.

His wife Helga was always with him. She was a delightful woman that reminded me of a picture I had once seen of a radiant Norwegian mother. She stood straight and sturdy at about 5'8, with two impeccably neat blonde braids, each pinned up against the sides of her head so they met at the top. She had a kind, sunny face and a heavy Norwegian accent. The news of her husband's need for surgery here in the U.S. had torn her from her comfortable home in Norway and separated her from close friends and family.

In this foreign land things moved quickly from bad to worse for her precious husband. Now Helga found herself here in the bustling city of Houston, in yet another hospital room, holding a solitary vigil for her dying husband.

When we met, I was impressed by her warm kindness and trusting acceptance of her husband's end of life time. She was the most pleasant, upbeat, confident woman I have ever met. I came to know her as a very intelligent woman that seemed to live in a place of total inner peace and natural joy. I fully enjoyed having her in the room.

Each day she was there from early morning to late evening. She filled her many empty hours by lovingly crocheting beautiful gifts for others and talking to her husband. She never interfered with my work and seemed to fill the room with sunshine. She was joyfully devoted to her husband. She wasn't syrupy or suffocating with her love. She was simply, confidently, completely in love.

The first day we met she told me that their children were coming for Christmas and that Papa John would be waking up in time for them to all spend one last Christmas together. This she knew even as she was fully aware of his tragic condition. Knowing he no longer had the bodily means to support his life here much longer, she knew that each day, each hour, was now a precious gift. She knew that he was at the very end of his lifetime. Still, she told any staff she came in contact with the same exciting news of their upcoming family Christmas.

Each day she would inform Papa John as to how many days were left until Christmas. It would be "Papa John, there's only five days left until Christmas! Remember, the children are coming! You have to wake up so we can all have one last Christmas together." She would happily remind him of this periodically throughout each day. Her faith and conviction were unwavering.

Personally, as a nurse, I have witnessed four patients awaken from a coma. It was thrilling and humbling at the same time. This life and these bodies that we are given are truly miraculous mysteries. However, according to modern medicine, Papa John's interior body was far too damaged to recover in any way. He would lie there unmoving, day after day, completely unresponsive, with those startling blue eyes staring up at us. I had to put drops in them regularly throughout my shift to keep them lubricated because he never even blinked.

Yet, despite his dire condition and close proximity to death, Helga remained convinced that he would wake up for one last family Christmas with her and their children. She never tried to defend her conviction or convince me or any others of her belief. It was simply an absolute fact in her mind. It was plain to see that she believed it with every cell of her being. Any part of her ego that might doubt this was completely dissolved.

At different times the hospital social worker and the chaplain visited her to offer support. They noted that her faith was unwavering, her trust complete. To me it was beautiful to behold. Even though this was deemed a medical impossibility, I have witnessed far too many miracles to doubt that it was possible. Consequently, I fully opened to the possibility of him awakening. I did not judge her as being irrational or in denial. We did not discuss her belief or his dire condition. Even at such a trying time her trust remained pure and she remained fully present. I could see that she actually felt him awakening.

That year I was flying home for the holidays. I was leaving after my shift on Christmas Eve day. When I entered Papa John's room that last morning, he was still lying corpse-like in his bed, still completely unresponsive. Helga, however, could barely contain her excitement! She 'knew' he would be awakening any time now. She had absolutely no doubt. It was as if the Divine had spoken to her directly and told her so. (This I could easily relate to as I am often given Divine messages myself.)

Excitedly she told him "Papa John, it's Christmas Eve morning! The children are on their way! It's time to wake up!"

She was such a joy, and her faith was contagious. Each day I had sent a little blessing to her and Papa John. I trusted that our Divine Source would do what was best for her and her family.

That morning, after receiving report on all my patients, checking on them and taking vital signs, I began their care. After attending to their morning medications, treatments, and other needs and getting them settled, I returned to Papa John. I carefully turned him onto his back, and tended to his hygiene and the many dressings and drains. All the while, his wife chatted excitedly to me. She was so enjoyable to be around! Once I completed this part of his care, I left them to check on my other patients and do further care. When that part of their care was complete and they were comfortable and content for the moment, I stopped to do my next regular check on Papa John.

Helga was absolutely glowing! She was so excited about his imminent return. Her unbridled love and joy were pure and palpable. She made no effort to contain her excitement about Papa John's return for Christmas. Again, she reminded him that it was time to wake up because the children were on their way. It lifted my spirits another notch whenever I was around her.

As for Papa John, he looked comfortable but had that gurgle again that signified he needed another quick suctioning. I told Helga I was going to suction him again, which she fully understood and was used to by now as this was a necessary treatment several times a shift. I went to the side of the bed and prepared my suction kit on my little elevated table as always. Once I had the suction catheter in my gloved hand ready to begin, I explained to Papa John that I was going to place the catheter in his nose and down to the back of his throat again to quickly clear it for him.

Even though he was always unresponsive, I explained the procedure to him each and every time before beginning to insert the catheter into his nose. It was my regular practice with all my patients to explain any procedures before I began so they would understand and not be taken by surprise. I then deftly slipped the lubricated catheter into his nostril. Helga happened to be standing close behind me at that moment. As the catheter slipped to the back of his throat to where I would begin suctioning, it happened!

Suddenly, a massively strong arm materialized, seemingly out of nowhere! It happened so fast; it did not compute! In a nanosecond my alarmed brain wondered where it had come from! My first thought was that some crazed person had been hiding under the bed, as it reached up, like an arm reaching up out of the grave, and grabbed my wrist in a near bone-crushing vice grip. I could barely believe it was real! In one quick motion it forcefully shoved my arm backwards, causing the suction catheter to come flying out of Papa John's nose!

In that same moment, this near corpse of a man suddenly commanded "Get that damned thing out of my nose!" I was so startled that I reflexively jumped back, bumping into his wife so hard that my 110 lbs. nearly knocked her over!

When I began to apologize to her, she was already in celebration mode. She was ecstatic! Her Papa John had come back for Christmas as she knew he would! As I worked to regain my composure, I turned back to him. The head of the bed was partially elevated and he was reclining there looking lovingly at Helga, who in a flash, had transported herself to the other side of the bed to be nearer to him. Clutching both of her hands in his, he was telling her "It's ok Mama, I'm here."

As I stood there with my heart nearly beating out of my chest, it was hard not to stare. This man that had been in a coma for so many months, whose body was riddled with wounds and so ravaged inside, was now awake and talking! He exuded a strength and sense of wellbeing that did not remotely match his internal physical condition. IIis fiery ice blue eyes were clear and bright. His voice was confident and deep and he was fully oriented and coherent as Helga introduced him to me. Strikingly handsome, he seemed to pulse with formidable strength and power. It was like Odin himself had dropped down from the Heavens! Yet despite his large commanding presence he was even tempered and pleasant. I liked him immediately.

I lingered for a bit, unwilling to take my eyes off of him while the full reality sunk in. As I stood rooted to the spot, still shell shocked, I listened to him speak about looking forward to seeing their children for Christmas. Although Papa John had the bold, towering presence of a fearless leader, the powerful love and tenderness between him and Helga was clearly visible. It filled the room.

The 'impossible' had happened once again and I was humbled to bear witness to yet another true miracle, or 'Divine intervention.'

Finally, I took my leave, allowing them precious time together. I tore my resistant feet from the room and headed out to the nursing station still somewhat numb from the sudden shock of what had transpired. I went to notify the doctor in charge of Papa John's care and share the amazing news. Unexpectedly, he happened to be standing there talking to one of the other nurses. I approached them and asked if he would come and take a quick look at Papa John for me.

"Why?" he asked. "Are his vital signs dropping? You know he is a 'do not attempt resuscitation" (which basically means should his heart stop or he stops breathing, we are not to take any measures to revive him)

"His vitals are stable" I replied.

"Well then what could you possibly need me for?" he asked. "Has one of his drains come out?"

"No. You just have to come see this to believe it. -Both of you."

"What is it?" he said, "Tell me."

"Well, you really need to see it," I said.

 "No. Now you have to tell me," He insisted.

"Ok. - He's awake."

"Impossible!" he cried.

"No!" blurted out my team mate. "He can't be!"

"He is," I said. "You have to come see for yourself."

"That's crazy!" the doctor said. "You've been working too much overtime!"

"Yes, I have," I said. "But Papa John is awake. Come see for yourself."

Reluctantly he and my coworker finally followed me back to Papa John's room, asking along the way if this was some kind of a joke.

"Be prepared." I said as we were about to enter the room. "He's sitting up talking with his wife."

As you might imagine, both the doctor and my coworker were shocked when they entered the room. The doctor literally stopped short in his tracks, temporarily at a loss for words after seeing Papa John now sitting up in bed conversing with his wife. I stepped around him and announced that he and the other nurse had come to say hello.

Soon after, as word spread of Papa John's miraculous awakening, the rest of the staff who had previously been concerned that Helga was going to be sadly disappointed, made their way to his room to witness this startling miracle.

As for myself, the rest of my shift passed joyfully. At the end of it I wished everyone a Merry Christmas and Happy Holiday and left to catch my plane. I was overflowing with happiness knowing that I had received one of the greatest Christmas gifts ever!

When I returned, after being away for a week, I heard of the happy reunion and wonderful Christmas that Helga and Papa John had with their grown children. Although Papa

John remained bed-bound he was happy, peaceful, and had enjoyed each moment with his family. He was even able to enjoy some tiny tastes of their Christmas feast. They all spent a joyful two days together. Then, after enjoying this last Christmas with his beloved wife and children, he closed his eyes and quietly passed on, completely infused with love.

Helga was gone from Houston when I returned. She had left me a special gift of gratitude; a tiny pair of sunshine yellow, perfectly crocheted and starched high heel shoes.

Little did she know that the brief time I spent with her and Papa John, witnessing the amazing love they shared, was one of the greatest gifts of my life.

Precious Reunion

Generally, I am not one to be regularly visited by spirits, but it does happen. More often when I have a visit with spirit it is when I 'cross thresholds' or change my state of consciousness by shifting into a higher state and connect with them. But sometimes they just show up.

After leaving the exciting city of Houston I moved to rural Alaska to work in a remote bush hospital. Although I had been looking forward to living and working in Alaska at some point, I was not yet ready to leave Houston. I had been enjoying my work and my life there and had planned to stay for another year or so. However, one morning as I was getting ready for work, I suddenly had a strong intuitive 'message' interrupt my thoughts. It was Divine guidance telling me that it was time to leave Houston and go to work in Alaska. I really loved my work and did not want to leave at that time. I asked if I could stay a few more months but the message was strong and clear: I was to give my notice at once. Reluctantly, I did as I was guided to do.

Now here I was a year later, standing alone in my friend Buck Turnbull's kitchen in rural Alaska, struggling over a tough personal decision I had made. I imagined that when I shared my choice with my mother, she would be upset. It was a decision with two tough sides and I had had to choose one.

As I stood working mindlessly at the counter, lost in my thoughts, my grandmother, who had died four years earlier, suddenly appeared. I gasped! There she was standing across from me on the other side of the counter! It was such a surprise to have her appear like that! My heart nearly burst! I love my grandmother deeply. Nearly every day throughout my childhood and into my adolescence I walked, often barefoot, down the quiet dirt road that connected our two homes to visit her. There she would patiently spend hours playing cards with me, listening to details of my day, or teaching me all sorts of things. Some of my favorites were baking and sewing. We would spend hours together, baking from scratch, creating the most amazing desserts that my grandfather, uncle, father and brothers very happily caused to disappear nearly as fast as we could bake them. It was so much fun!

Sewing, however, was my favorite. When she taught me to sew, first by hand, and then on her machine, a magical world of creation opened up to me. I first began making clothes for my doll, and by junior high I was creating my own clothes, including prom gowns.

In all of our time together I felt very connected, completely peaceful, and totally loved. Her death had been a tremendous blow to me and I missed her terribly.

Now she was here again! My heart was nearly bursting with love as she stood before me so straight and beautiful. She looked so much younger, completely at ease, and full of peace. She had suffered with MS and rheumatoid arthritis and had been hunched over in life. Now she stood straight and solidly on both legs (one of her legs had been amputated a year before she died). I could not move or take my eyes off of her.

I imagined that she would have been very disappointed in my aforementioned choice as well. I silently communicated to her that I was so very sorry to disappoint her. However, she surprised me by very distinctly telling me (again in a wordless, telepathic communication) that it was completely fine, without question, no judgment. I felt her limitless love and her unwavering confidence and support of me. It was an incredibly precious reunion.

She stayed with me some wonderful moments, and then she was gone, back into my heart.

Laura Blue

After leaving Alaska I took a few months off and went to live in South America for a while with my close high school friend Buffy and her husband, Tom. They were both teaching school and living in Ecuador with their two-year-old son Jeffrey. Buffy was also nearly nine months pregnant when I arrived. She had her first child here in the US and was somewhat apprehensive about giving birth in a strange hospital, in a foreign land, with no other family around. We were both very happy that I was able to fly down to be with her.

My beautiful friend was very active and absolutely glowed with good health. The day she went into labor, I was amazed at how well she managed it. She, her husband and I walked across a large park to catch a cab to the hospital. Once she was settled into bed however, her contractions stopped and she was happy for the time-out as she was now nearly exhausted. Her doctor came and sat beside her bed and explained that they would induce her (this meant using intravenous medication to stimulate her uterus to begin the contractions of labor) if her labor did not begin again soon. As he sat there chatting with her, a sense of unease began growing in me. Then I 'received a message' that her baby needed to be born ASAP, that she did not have time to wait to be induced. This message came in the form of a sudden knowing inside my head, which interrupted my thoughts, along with a very distressed feeling in my own body. I knew I had to act quickly. It was as if the baby was sending out an S.O.S. (there was no fetal monitor).

The doctor and I did not know each other and I was certain he would not take me seriously. Thankfully, he left the room after what seemed like an eternity of idle chit chat but was really only a couple of moments. I immediately told my friend that she had to get up out of bed and walk around a bit to stimulate her labor, (as walking sometimes can.) I told her she needed to have this baby NOW. She looked at me like I had lost my mind. She was feeling completely spent and was so very comfortable in the bed. I was gentle but firm, and I wasn't giving up. After a couple of minutes, she begrudgingly agreed to a few steps and she let me help her up. (I think she only agreed to do it so I would then let her rest!)

Part of me felt terrible for insisting that my exhausted, pregnancy-laden friend go to such great effort to move her now enormous belly out of the comfort of the bed, and lug it across the room. However, I knew how imperative it was that she jump-start her labor at once. As she took a few steps, her labor immediately returned with a vengeance and by the time she was back in bed she was ready for the delivery room. Her husband and I accompanied her, and within moments of arriving in delivery, we witnessed the exhilarating miracle of new life!!!

Except...........

There was no first breath.

No first sound.

All was silent...

My heart nearly stopped when I saw that this perfectly formed baby girl was completely blue! Her entire silent, perfect little body hung limp and unmoving in the doctor's outstretched hands. She looked like a beautiful, tiny, lifeless alien. The cord was wrapped twice around her neck, cutting off her oxygen, causing her to be that beautiful, potentially deadly shade of blue that all of us who know better, dread.

The doctor acted quickly. He removed and cut the cord and in seconds began trying to revive her. Then, going on instinct, I was about to grab the newborn from his hands and rush her to the oxygen when the doctor jumped up and ran her over to it himself.

Thankfully, she began breathing right away. Her skin 'pinked up' (her normal color returned) and finally, with a strong wail, she announced herself to the world. Now I 'knew' all was well, both from a sense of comfort and total peace, as well as a very clear 'knowing.'

Once again, being fully present allowed me to notice the changing feelings in my body and allowed the message to come through.

*Now, years later, a perfectly healthy, lovely young woman walks the earth shining her own light wherever she goes.

Uncle Robert

It was the rare occasion that my Uncle Robert was not there to drive me to physical therapy three times a week after a debilitating auto accident that completely changed my life. I had recently returned to Massachusetts from Ecuador when the accident occurred. His never-ending love and support had seen me through many an impossible spot. It was his love that carried me through the first years after the accident.

Then, one day, he was gone. He died suddenly one Sunday morning after having a deadly heart condition overlooked in the ER just two days earlier.

I was staying at my parent's house and my mother came to get me. One of my older brothers was asleep downstairs but no one else was home. She was wide eyed and restless and said she knew something was wrong because my uncle hadn't stopped by with the Sunday paper. Unrelenting pain from multiple injuries consumed me and I was severely restricted physically, but she was so extremely anxious that I let her take me next door with her to his home. When we arrived, his door, which would normally be unlocked at this time, was still locked. When he didn't answer my mother's frantic knocking, she unlocked it. (She had taken her key with her because she so strongly felt that something was terribly wrong.) After entering we saw that his little dog, Felina was running around barking, and that my uncle wasn't in the kitchen or living room. Something was dreadfully wrong.

My uncle loved to sit out on the big enclosed front porch each day and evening and look out at nature. He loved watching the trees and flowers, and the birds and animals, as well as the changes each new day and evening would bring. It was here that we found him. He was in his favorite spot on the glider, slumped over sideways. His eyes were open with a soft, far away glow, and the lower side of his face was purple. He had been dead awhile. It was such a tremendous shock! My poor heart broke wide open! Blistering pain exploded out of my mother like a suddenly burst dam, as she began screaming at me to do CPR. (Even as she knew I couldn't possibly have done it in my condition.) I was shocked myself and crying out my grief, between trying to tell her that he was already gone. Then, in a frenzy of massive shock and grief she began running wildly in and out of the room crying and screaming uncontrollably.

I somehow managed to call into my parent's answering machine for my older brother Jimmy to come right away. He did. Somehow, the police were called and my brother helped console my mother and spoke with the police.

While we waited for the undertaker, the police officers kept coming out on the porch trying to coax me away from my uncle's body. I kept telling them that I knew he was gone, but this would be the last time I could be near him in this way and I wanted to stay with his body until the undertaker came. Despite their best efforts to convince me otherwise, I remained with him. I knew it was their own discomfort that made them want me to leave the porch. They were very caring police officers.

My Uncle Robert was my mother's brother. They grew up very close and remained that way. They were always there for each other through hard times and good times. He and my Father were very close as well. He was like a second father/best friend to me. Growing up I spent countless hours sitting on the porch with him. He was a sanctuary of unconditional love and acceptance. A true lover of nature, a great source of comfort and support in hard times, and a living embodiment of kindness and compassion.

I would not have come through the times of being terrorized in my childhood if not for him. Even though I never told him exactly what I endured, his love and his taking time to sit with me got me through. I thank God every day for my time here with him.

One day, a few months after he died, he came to me in a lucid dream. It was as real as in waking-life. In the 'dream' I had just returned to my hometown for a visit with friends and family after one of my many journeys. After spending some time with my parents, I walked down the lane to his house. I could hardly wait to see him! When I knocked, he soon opened the door just as he had a thousand times before. Not expecting me, (I loved to surprise him and my grandfather with a visit whenever I could) he was thoroughly overjoyed to see me. He excitedly ushered me in and swept me up in a great big, loving hug. He exuded pure, unconditional love and complete joy! Besides feeling a powerful surge of genuine love, I could feel the solid strength of his arms and chest, smell his familiar clean smell, and hear his voice. I experienced him just as if he were still alive and I was really standing in his kitchen being hugged by him. It was as solid and real an experience as if I were to hug you right now. In this expanded space, as always, he was so happy to see me. He let me know that he was beyond delighted in his new phase of life, that Heaven was all he knew it would be, and so much more. He let me know that our bond of love could never be broken, and that he is still here with me always.

After what seemed like endless moments, I 'awoke' back in my bed completely filled with love, joy and gratitude. So much so that it felt as if each tiny cell in my body were completely filled with these wonderful feelings.

I am so very blessed!

Shifting Energy

One day, while living in Massachusetts, I was sitting on my couch relaxing, reading a book, when suddenly, a high school friend's name came charging into my head! I hadn't had a thought about him in several years. Then, every day for a few weeks, once a day, the same thing would happen. I could be reading, watching TV, in the middle of a conversation, or lost in my sculpting. It didn't matter. Suddenly, out of the blue, he would come blasting into my thoughts, unannounced, like a news flash. At once I knew something was up but I had no idea where he (Robbie) was or how to contact him. Then one day I was going through the line at the grocery store and the cashier looked at me and said "I know you. You're Sharon Saulenas. You don't know me but we have a mutual friend." She went on to tell me that she was a close friend of Robbie's. I asked how he was. She closed her cash register, pulled me aside and told me that he had recently had brain surgery for a deadly brain tumor and was told that he only had three months to live. You can imagine my shock and sorrow at hearing this. She gave me his number and hoped I would call him.

I was saddened to hear of his illness and wanted to see him before he died. We had an unusual friendship throughout high school. He was in and out of school and I didn't see much of him. When I did, he was bubbly and fun and respectful of the fact that I had a steady boyfriend. Somehow, we became good friends.

When I first met him, I was standing in the hall in high school after class talking to my boyfriend and his friend. At one point another student came around the corner and was walking down the hall in our direction. I was facing his way, watching him as he walked toward us. Then I was staring, because what I now know to be his aura, suddenly burst out around him! It was a great, large cloud of golden light that filled and surrounded him. More than that, at the same time I suddenly 'knew' him. I 'knew' that we had known each other in other lifetimes - in many lifetimes! We had been lovers and spouses in various lives! I also 'knew' that was not our destiny for this lifetime. I was shocked and speechless! Up until then I had not seen a human aura or recognized anyone from another time!

(I learned a strange thing many years later. Robbie and I had both been born the same year, in the same month, on the same day, at the same time! Our parents, who never met, moved to the town we grew up in when we were both the same young age.)

At home I told my boyfriend at the time, (I'll call him Doug) about my meeting in the supermarket. He knew Robbie was an old friend and encouraged me to call him. In my heart I knew it was the beginning of another big shift for me and that Doug would not do well with it. I was two years out of my spontaneous healing from a traumatic brain injury and other debilitating injuries and Doug and I were not doing well. He was unable to support my newly enhanced abilities and constantly told me not to talk about any of it because people would think that I was a freak. He was also always worried that my recovery would wear off and I would revert back to being crippled again.

There was much fear. I felt stifled and he felt he needed to protect me. We tried to work it out but were unsuccessful. After his continued refusals to try counseling, I told him I needed a separation and had begun looking for the best way to do so. I now felt very strongly that somehow, once I made the phone call to Robbie, it would start something from which there was no turning back. So, I hesitated for a few days. Three days later I made the call. It was great to speak with him after such a long time! He invited me up to his home in Maine for a visit. I mentioned it to my mother and she wanted to come along. She had always liked him and felt terrible about his diagnosis. So we went up and found him lying on his back porch, sunning his face. I hadn't seen him in many years. He was fit but had a sickly grey tinge to his skin. I could tell it was somewhat of an effort for him to be his usual buoyant self but he was very glad to see us both.

Near the end of our visit, I was drawn to offer healing to him. I explained some of the work I do and asked if I could balance his energy. He said he didn't think he could sit still for 10 minutes or even 5. Some of the medications he was on made him a bit jittery. However, he finally agreed to try and sit for just one minute. That's all it took.

When he stood up, my mother was shocked and commented on how the color in his face had improved. He said he felt peaceful, lifted and refreshed. We made plans to meet again to talk about Hospice.

The following are a few of the wondrous experiences that Robbie and I shared...

Headache Relief

Shortly after I began visiting Robbie, he started having crushing headaches from Glioblastomas, a deadly type of brain tumor.

It's a ruthless cancer that infiltrates the brain. He had recently had brain surgery to reduce as much of the bulk of the tumors as possible in order to give him temporary relief since they could not actually remove them. Now these two wretched masses were growing again, taking up space and causing inflammation as they grew, putting more and more pressure on his brain, hoping to gradually squeeze it out of its rightful seat within his skull.

The first time I witnessed these headaches, he was lying on the couch consumed by unspeakable pain. This was a very tough man that had been in many physical battles in his lifetime. Once he had been attacked and slashed multiple times with a knife and left to die. No matter what, he always pulled through. Now he was living with two deadly tumors that were crushing his brain more each day, causing excruciating pain as they committed to ending his life. Today he had no control over himself or the pain.

When I arrived, he was moaning loudly and thrashing around wildly on the couch, the pain having taken over. I turned to my higher wisdom and asked what I could do, if anything to help him. Suddenly I was given a 'message' (as a sudden knowing) to put my hand on his head. As I attempted to do so, he immediately flung my hand away and continued moaning and thrashing side to side. He was, understandably, unable to tolerate being touched, even lightly at this point. So, I now kept my hand just above his head and followed his head with my hand as best I could. Immediately I began to feel heat coming into my hand. I kept following his head and the heat kept coming, like I was pulling it out of his head. My hand grew warmer and warmer. At one point my hand was so hot, it was almost unbearable, like being held too close to a hot burner or flame. It took all I could do to stay with it. Soon I noticed he was not thrashing around and moaning as much. As I 'pulled' more and more heat out, his distress decreased. Just as I wondered how much longer I could stand the now very intense heat, it seemed that it was complete. Heat stopped coming out of his head and I removed my hand. My palm felt terribly hot, like it was burned, but thankfully it cooled very quickly!

Robbie had stopped moving and moaning. He then sat up and looked at me and asked, "How did you do that?" I knew that I hadn't 'done' anything myself, that Divine healing had come through me. I told him it was the Divine acting through me. He looked intently at me for a moment and then thanked me. Then he said, "I'm starving. Want to go get lunch?" - and we did! Once again, I was amazed and grateful.

For the next three months, he had no need for pain medication when I was with him. Each time he began to get the crushing pain, I would put my hand on his head and 'pull' heat out and the pain would be gone; even after he went into the hospital at the end of his life. He spent only one week in the hospital, something his brain surgeon could hardly believe.

One day I left his hospital room to take a short walk outside. When I returned, he was in terrible pain and his nurse had gone to get pain medication for him. As his sister looked on, I placed my hand on his head and the pain was gone before the nurse returned. This was just days before he passed.

Even as he had some major deficits from the effects of the brain tumor, his brain surgeon and other doctors could not believe that he had been up and about, going to lunch and working out at the gym everyday with such large tumors in his brain right up until a week before he was hospitalized.

In order to help him, rather than get caught up in feelings of pity, anxiety or sorrow, I remained centered, allowing guidance and healing to come through.

Uninvited Guest

One night I stayed over at Robbie's house. The house was over 100 years old and he had told me earlier that he had seen the ghost of a woman a few times and it had really freaked him out. This night I was in one of the unused bedrooms upstairs when I began to have some sort of dream experience where I knew I was dreaming. I was doing some very difficult type of work that required tremendous effort and energy expenditure on my part. It wasn't really clear what the work was, but I felt I was struggling with every ounce of my strength to get free in some way. It was quite rigorous. I felt as if I was being pulled further and further down into some deep, dark place. It was as if someone had a hold on my ankles and wanted to keep me captive down there. The force was incredibly strong and I was struggling and fighting with every bit of my strength to get free.

After a while, I began to wear down. I could feel my strength draining away and knew I couldn't fight it off much longer. Then I remembered that I was of the Divine. I called for Divine assistance and surrendered. I woke up.

It was the middle of the night and I was sweating, shaking all over, and feeling spent and unsettled. I had been lying on my side and when I opened my eyes, there was a 'ghost' of a woman lying a couple of feet from me. She was also lying on her side with her back towards me. I could see every detail of her hair and clothes - just as if it had been you lying there. She was such a surprise! Normally I would have stayed and opened communication but I was so intensely jangled by the dream experience that I really needed to shake it off. I got up and went downstairs to the bathroom, splashed cold water on my face and got a drink of water. I took some time to center myself. Robbie heard me and came to see if I was all right. I asked him to sit with me for a few minutes because I felt so unsettled. After a few minutes I was fine. I told him about the dream experience that had no clear story or visual.

Now I was wide awake, calmed and centered, so I went back upstairs and laid down. Within a moment or two of lying down, the woman reappeared. She had rich, straight brown hair and was about my height and weight. The unusual thing was that she looked nearly completely like a real person lying there. There was just something missing. She looked solid but yet not. I could easily tell she was in spirit form. I looked at her for a while, taking in the details of her spirit. Then I 'asked' what she had come for. I did not have to speak aloud. She replied by thanking me, telepathically, for helping her and finally setting her free. With this I could feel myself fill with her soft loving gratitude. It felt delightful...like being filled with a smile! In the next moment she was gone. I now understood that the earlier struggle had somehow been for her. Robbie came to check on me a few moments later and I told him what had happened. He was shocked when I described the woman. He said she was the one he had seen before in the house a few times.

Neither of us ever saw her again.

Sharing Space

As I previously mentioned, I assisted my dear friend Robbie through his end-of-life process. One of his regrets was that he had not been able to visit his mother before she died and that things had been left unsaid. This weighed heavily on him.

As we returned to his home late one evening, he expressed this to me again. I reminded him that just as we pray and talk to Source, he could still talk to his mother and let her know how he felt since we remain connected always, even after death. I then stepped out of the dark, frigid cold and into the welcoming warmth of the house. He opted to remain in the backyard to speak to her and let her know how he felt.

Soon after, an eerie sound floated in from outside where the pitch-black Maine woods stood all around us. My skin crawled as I listened to what sounded like a badly wounded animal. As I wondered what type of animal it was and where it might be, the sound grew louder. Suddenly I realized it was human and it was coming from Robbie! As I started to the door, it opened and he stumbled in. A deep, deep, mournful wail that seemed to originate in the depths of his being was pouring out of him. It was almost unearthly. Chills ran through me as I listened to such bottomless grief. On instinct, I started to step closer to comfort him. However, just before I did, his mother suddenly appeared (her essence) off to my right. I wasn't totally surprised as we both had been feeling her presence for the past few days. My real surprise came when she wordlessly (by mental telepathy) asked if she might share my body in order to communicate with her son! As odd as that may seem there was something, at the same time, vaguely familiar about it. It was if I had done this before.

At once, the ancient wisdom that seems to come forth from the back of my skull informed me that this was something I have done before and could do now. In that moment I decided to trust and consented. Barely finishing my thought, she was instantly in my body! I experienced it as if 'I' moved over and she was beside 'me', each taking up one half of my body. At once an explosion of joy and unconditional love filled me! It was if I was filled with bright sunshine! I remember that my mouth automatically went into a full joyful smile. She then walked my body across the kitchen and embraced her son who continued his mournful wailing. With my arms she embraced him. Using my words, she told him she loved him and that everything was all right. He then shocked me by saying "I love you too Mom". I was stunned! He said MOM!!! He Knew!!! The terrible wailing had now reduced to soft weeping. She held him, and kissed him and then stepped back. In a flash she was gone and I filled out my bodily space again. To say I was completely amazed would be an understatement. I was blown away! I was so humbled that I could be a vehicle for love in this way.

Robbie then crossed the room, slid down the wall and sat on the floor still weeping softly. I went over and sat beside him and put my arm around his shoulder. After a time, we got up and sat on the couch. My mind was racing inside wondering what the experience had been like for him, but I sat quietly nearby nearly bursting at the seams. Finally, when he stopped weeping, I asked him what that was all about. In a soft hushed voice he replied, "That was my mother holding me in the kitchen. She told me she loved me and let me know everything is all right. Then it was just you holding me when I was on the floor." Again, I was astounded!!! I would never have imagined any of it in a million years! We both just sat there for a while, absorbing it all. Later we talked more about it.

For a while I had no idea why these things happened. I just continued to practice trust in our Divine Source, staying open and willing to be a tool for healing in whatever form it takes. I can't tell you that it's always easy, but overall, I feel totally safe, supported, and loved.

Uncle Marcy

One year I began the New Year house-sitting a couple of days for my dear friend Joan.

I had just gotten into bed and was lying there in an odd kind of funky mood, wondering if I was truly on the right path and what the New Year would bring. I had let go of so much in my life to devote myself more fully to my Inner Guidance. Suddenly, as I was contemplating all of this, my Uncle Marcy (who had died a few months earlier) materialized in the bedroom doorway! He nearly took my breath away as he appeared so suddenly and unexpectedly and was so life-like! He looked as he had in pictures I had seen of him as a very young man. Casually leaning against the doorframe in a white t-shirt and jeans, he appeared totally relaxed and completely self-assured. His stance reminded me of pictures I had seen of an old American heartthrob named James Dean. As he stood smiling at me, radiating love and happiness, in a wordless mental telepathy he let me know that I was all right, I was on the right track, and that he loved me. At once, immense joy and unconditional love filled me. It filled me to overflowing!

He stayed a few moments with me, looking at me with such loving admiration and unbounded love, and then he was gone. Later, besides feeling very blessed by his visit, I thought about how I could always tell as a child that he loved me very much. The feeling was mutual. I did not see him very often growing up. However, even if we were not in direct contact, I remember always feeling that he loved me as if I were one of his own children. He was strict, and I would not describe him as an outwardly spiritual man, yet I always felt his love loud and clear.

Rocky Road

Near the end of his life, my father developed respiratory disease. The further it progressed, the more frequent the hospitalizations for respiratory distress became as is, unfortunately, most often the case. I loved my father dearly and it was always heartbreaking to see him struggle for air. I wanted to help but he did not want help at that time. Although difficult, I had to honor his wishes.

One day as I was preparing to leave for a conference in Austin, Texas, my mother called to tell me that my father had been admitted to the hospital again and was told that he had pneumonia in one lung. This was especially serious with his lung disease.
As soon as I was able, I went to visit him and helped him relax.

I was due to leave town the next day and wondered how I could leave with him being so ill. It was very distressing so I took some deep breaths and 'checked in' with my Inner Wisdom. The 'message' came through that although my father would have a rocky road, he would survive. He was comforted knowing that I was given the 'message' that he was going to be ok. I gave him my love, and left the following morning as planned.

Two days after arriving in Texas, however, I received a phone call from my terribly frightened mother. She anxiously told me that my father now had pneumonia in both lungs and that his doctor was giving him only a 50/50 chance of survival.

Again, fear clutched at me but I took some deep breaths and decided to trust in the message I had received earlier. I 'checked in' again to see what I could do to help, if anything. This time I was given the message to do a long-distance healing with him. This was something I had not previously done and I was a little apprehensive. However, the complete support of the wonderful new friends I had met at the conference lifted me, and as always, I chose to trust. I stopped and took some deep breaths and called my cousin who was at the hospital visiting my father at the time. I asked her to ask him if he would like to do some healing on the phone. He agreed. I asked her to assist him. I told her to let my father know that I would call back later that day at a certain time (which I felt was the right time), and asked if she could please be there to assist him. She agreed. We hung up and I went to my conference.

Later that afternoon, I made the call to my father's room and my cousin answered as planned. Since he was so ill and very weak, I asked her to hold the phone for him while I worked with him, and when we were done, he would let her know and she could hang up. She was to then draw the curtain around his bed to let him rest and then come back and check on him in about 10-15 minutes.

Sitting holding my hotel phone in one hand and the curly phone cord in the other, I began channeling healing energy to my father. Immediately I was surprised at how the cord began to come alive with energy! This continued as I spoke to him. Then, at one point I got a visual of what reminded me of Pac Man characters moving along gobbling up what appeared to be the infection in my Father's lung! This showed itself on a big 'screen' that suddenly materialized across the room in the air in front of me. I was so surprised! It was so bizarre yet at the same time it seemed to be an effective metaphor for the healing that was taking place. I decided to continue to trust and accept it. So I enjoyed the strange scene as I continued. Then it was complete. The 'screen' disappeared and I told my father we were done. I told him I loved him and asked him to rest and I would check on him later.

That evening when I was done for the day, I called my cousin at the designated time. She was so excited she was bubbling over. I had to ask her to slow down so I could understand all she was saying. She reported that she had been very, very frightened earlier that day when she first went in to see my father. She said, "He was a scary grey color and was noticeably exhausted." She went on to say, "He was coughing and coughing and having such a difficult time breathing that he could not engage in conversation. He was fighting exhaustively for each breath. He could not rest back in bed even with the head of the bed elevated and had to sit on the edge of the bed and lean on his bedside table for support." She went on about how very ill and worn out he was and how terrible he looked and sounded. Later, she had done as I instructed. She had left the room after the long-distance healing and then returned to check on him.

Barely able to contain her joy and excitement, she rushed on to describe what she found when she returned to look in on him, "I could hardly believe my eyes! He was back in bed, quietly resting with the head of the bed up about 3/4 of the way. The color in his face shocked me as well!
The grey had disappeared and although he was pale, his color looked more normal to me. He had finally dozed off. There was no more coughing or desperate struggling for each breath!"

She had stayed for a while watching him then left him sleeping peacefully.

The next day my mother called to tell me that my Father's X-ray showed the pneumonia was completely gone in one lung and much improved in the other. He was feeling much better as well. Three days later he was home.

Once again, by trusting and staying present, I was able to assist with healing...even long distance!

Refocusing

One beautiful summer day, my kindhearted friend Annmarie called and asked if I could come by and see her neighbor, a young man we both knew. She was very upset because he was sitting in her kitchen crying inconsolably. He had been there over an hour and she didn't know what to do. He was depressed over his girlfriend leaving him and he had not gone to work or eaten for a couple of days. She had offered to call his doctor or therapist but he refused. Frightened and worried about him, she called and asked if I would come see him as he had agreed to talk to me.

When I arrived, the poor guy looked so beaten down. Slumped into her kitchen chair, his hair was mussed and his clothes disheveled. His eyes were red and swollen and wet with tears. Besides feeling so terribly low he complained of an intense headache. I suggested that it might disappear if he had something to drink and eat. He insisted that he could not because he was nauseous. After speaking to him for a few minutes, I made an agreement with him. I asked him if he would drink some water and eat lunch if I could help him get rid of his nausea and headache. He didn't believe this was possible. However, after some gentle convincing and explaining how simple it would be, he agreed to try.

I centered myself and asked for guidance. I could then 'see' that a bunch of his energy was stuck up around his head.

We pulled up two chairs and I had him sit across from me. After describing again what we would be doing, I instructed him to focus in a certain way while moving his legs a certain way, as he made a particular sound at the same time. Less than five minutes later the headache was completely gone, as was the nausea. He was totally surprised. Now his focus was no longer on his great feeling of loss.

I was then given the 'message' that it was important to demonstrate to him that it was he, himself, who was in control of how he felt. I explained that to him and had him reverse the process. Immediately the headache and nausea returned with a vengeance. We then repeated the first process and once again he became pain and nausea free. He could hardly believe his experience! Since he was feeling much better, he drank some water and then ate lunch as agreed. He also agreed to call his counselor. Annmarie followed up with him and reported that he had sought professional help and was doing much better.

Eye Can Do This

One day I was involved in a freak accident where a large solid block of hard plastic, at the end of a tightly coiled spring, let go and smashed me in the face. It knocked me down and nearly knocked me unconscious. The pain was so blindingly intense I was certain I had lost my eye. I had to scream to keep the energy of the pain from knocking me out. My husband Kevin was in a panic! After helping me up and reassuring me that my eye was still there, he kept pacing back and forth saying, "What should I do? What should I do?".

He continued pacing and repeating this while I sat rocking and screaming out loudly in pain. He did think to call 911 or drive me to the hospital but when he said it, suddenly I got a very strong 'message' of "No, not yet." So, as you might imagine, he was quite frantic.

After a few moments of this however, he began listening to his own Inner Wisdom and suddenly stopped pacing. He surprised me by very forcefully saying, "Sharon, do what you do! You can stop this pain! Just do what you do!" This he repeated a few times in a very confident, authoritative voice. It took me a minute or so to focus and follow his directive because I was so overwhelmed by pain. Then I connected to Divine Source and was 'told' what to do. I was given a clear 'message' to put my hand over my eye. When I went to do it however, my hand just lightly brushed the tip of my nose. I nearly passed out from the increased intensity of the pain! I took a few deep breaths… in between screaming and crying… and put my hand over my eye again but this time without touching it or my nose. I held it there for what might have been a few minutes. I was still screaming and crying in unbearable pain. Kevin was standing nearby, bravely trusting the process. Then I 'got' that it was done and removed my hand. When I did, a solid 'beam' of energy came out of the center of my eye and continued to come out. It was palpable and long, and about as big around as a broom handle. This continuous beam stretched out in front of me, making its way steadily across the long length of the room. Still coming out of my eye, when it came to the end of the room and reached the wall, it continued on through the wall and out into the porch, then across it, and out the far wall into the outdoors. I felt a slight pull as the 'end' came out of my eye. It continued on its path across the room and out of the house and then it was done. As it was leaving, I felt the pain becoming more and more tolerable, less and less painful. When it was all the way out, the pain was gone - <u>completely</u>!!! Kevin had watched silently as I went from rocking and screaming in pain to becoming perfectly comfortable.

I don't know exactly what would have happened if he hadn't stopped and listened to his own inner voice, his Divine guidance. I do know that I would have been in the ER getting incredibly large amounts of pain medication!

He did take me to see my doctor. I was slightly off balance when I walked and my thoughts felt slowed for a couple of days. I was diagnosed with a concussion and an X-ray showed that I had two broken bones around my eye (which my doctor told me had saved me from losing my eye). My face and nose swelled up HUGE, with much of my face becoming black and blue, disfiguring it for a couple of weeks. Even so, I never did have any more pain. My doctor and my friends were absolutely amazed by this. I could even sleep soundly on that side without any pain!

I hope this experience reminds you of the powerful ability we all possess to heal ourselves. These physical bodies of ours are very real and at the same time made up of energy. At our core we are all energy.... pure vibrating essence.

Science has proven this.

Getting in touch with our higher consciousness, the place where we are all connected, where we are all One, brings us beyond our physical experience. It is here that healing easily takes place.

However, this physical plane is so alluring. Focusing on the drama of life around us pulls us away from our center, the inner, higher, true version of ourselves... our core essence where we are all highly vibrating energy connected to, and One with, all others. The truly wonderful thing is that we all have access to this Divine space. It simply takes trust and focusing inward. A regular practice of detaching from judgment and drama, staying fully present, and spending time each day turning inward is most helpful.

Choose to stay present in each moment. Catch yourself when you slip out and go back. Just keep bringing yourself back to the moment. Commit to these simple practices and you will experience more of the wonders of life and of your true self!

Kevin's Joyful Message

Late one morning, shortly before I experienced a life-changing visit to Heaven, I had an incredibly unique message from my late husband Kevin. During the few months since he had passed on, I had been going through massive waves of grief that felt like they would surely drown me. Today was a 'good' day. I had my head just up above it, feeling like I was at least treading water in it.

I was sitting on our couch, awake but resting, when Kevin reached out to me. His presence appeared in the air across from me, and up a little to the left in the living room, like he was hovering there. I had no visual but I could clearly feel him there; He 'spoke' to me (in a telepathic way). He was very excited and his energy was so very loving and joyful. It was like he was bubbling over and could barely wait to tell me the good news; that I was going to marry again! He was so very happy and just delighted with who I would marry. Then a 'screen' appeared beside him (beside where I felt his essence) where he began to list my future husband's attributes!

I was so shocked and he was so happy for me! He wanted me to be happy and go on and be loved again. I began reading down the list as he put them out there and then I stopped reading, turned away, and told him that it was too soon. I told him I wasn't against what he was sharing with me, just that it was too soon! I told him he must understand that I was still crushed from missing him and that I needed some time to heal first. He acknowledged that he understood and honored my wishes with his caring, compassionate nature. The screen then dissolved away as he bid me a very sweet, loving goodbye.

My head was almost spinning. I couldn't even attempt a thought of having another lover at that time while I was feeling so exhausted and broken open by Kevin's passing.

A couple of days later I called my dear friend, Mary St. Pierre. Mary and her husband Matthew are two of the most caring, compassionate people I know. Mary is also a very gifted Intuitive and Healer. She too has helped many individuals heal and experience inner peace. Mary and Kevin had a very close connection. They both felt they had known each other in a whole other lifetime rather than just these few years. Mary helped Kevin a great deal in his last few months here.

I wanted to share my 'visit' with her. I began by describing how Kevin had 'shown up' in our living room. Then I told her of his surprising message and how happy he was for me, and how unready I felt to receive it. I went on to tell her that Kevin was very pleased with this person that I am to marry and that he began to describe his characteristics with a list! I said "Mary, I'm just not ready to take it all in. It's too soon. I just can't imagine anyone other than Kevin right now."

I began to tell her what he listed. I got to the third thing on the list when she interrupted and began telling me the rest of what I saw. She finished the list with the exact same information in the exact same order! At first, I was shocked! Then I remembered it was Mary, after all, that I was talking to. She said "Sharon, I'm so very sorry. I wanted to call you the other day but Matthew thought it would be too much for you just yet. He knows how hard it is for you right now and thought it best to wait a bit."

Mary had the same 'visit' with the same list from Kevin on the very same day as I did! She went on to say that she was so relieved that I called because she wasn't sure she could hold off from telling me much longer. Then she said "I can even tell you what he looks like."

"No! Please, not yet!" I said. "I just can't go there yet."

So, I went on with my life, about to have one of the most extraordinary life changing experiences, as well as some of the deepest, most difficult challenges.

Perfumed Powder

One day my friend Sue had asked to have her first healing energy session. We got together one afternoon and began. Soon after, I was aware of her Father being present. I had never met him but I could strongly feel his essence, like when you can feel someone is in the room with you, even before you see them.

I continued to channel the energy. At one point I became aware of her Father leaving. Then, near the end of the session, an elderly woman suddenly materialized on my right side kneeling next to me on the pillow I was kneeling on. I could at once smell a very strong smell of perfume. Except that it wasn't perfume, it was a heavy smell of perfumed powder. At once I 'knew' that she was Sue's mother, and that she had something to relay to Sue. Suddenly part of a prayer began to play loudly and clearly in my head, over and over - "Blessed art thou among women, and blessed is the fruit of thy womb, Jesus." Then it switched to "Forgive us our trespasses as we forgive those who trespass against us. Lead us not into temptation, but deliver us from evil, Amen." This too played over and over for a minute or so. Then it stopped and her mother was gone. I knew these were messages that my friend would understand.

When we finished, Sue told me that her Father (whom she had unfinished business with) had come to her early on in the session and that she was able to converse with him for a while. She was so very happy with this because she now felt at peace with him. It was a very emotional experience for her. She began to wonder why her Mother hadn't come as well. When she finished describing her whole experience, I told her about the woman who had appeared beside me. As soon as I told her about the smell of the powder, she started laughing and crying at the same time! She told me that she and her sister used to joke about how much scented powder her Mother would use near the end of her life. When they cleaned out her room, even her dresser drawers had powder in them. She knew without a doubt, by the description and the powder that it was her mother who had visited.

I then told her about the pieces of prayers and how they were emphasized with constant repetition. At once she could relate the messages in them to struggles she was having in her life and immediately felt more clarity and gratitude.

Earth Angels

I love the term 'Earth Angel'.

Some of us use it to describe someone who was there, selflessly helping, supporting, or inspiring us just when we needed them.
They knowingly or unknowingly brighten someone's day.
The wonderful thing is that we all have the ability to be one!
Anytime we reach out to another to help or support them with no thought of acknowledgement or payment of any kind, we are living in our 'Earth Angel' energy.

Whenever you do even a small act of kindness for a friend, stranger, or any part of this world or it's inhabitants, you are living in your 'Earth Angel' energy.

There are limitless opportunities for this such as:

- o Shopping for a homebound caregiver
- o Adopting a stray dog or cat
- o Opening and holding a door for someone who is struggling
- o Shoveling an elderly or infirm neighbor's walk
- o Feeding birds during frigid weather
- o Sending a holiday card to someone who lives alone
- o Being polite and nonjudgmental,
- o Planting a flower or a tree, etc., etc., etc.

The really wonderful thing is that you may have a much larger impact on someone's life than you will ever know!

Frozen

The ground was blanketed deep with snow and a top coating of ice that mid-winter day. The roads had been recently plowed but they hadn't been sanded yet and were a slick sheet of ice. There were only a few rare cars on the road. My friends and I had decided to walk to the store. It was a brilliantly cold day and we were walking nearly single file, finding traction was best near the snow banks. We were well dressed against the sharp cold and at 15, I was enjoying just being out slipping and sliding along the road with a group of my friends.

Up ahead, a lone car rounded the corner moving too fast for the conditions. Suddenly it began sliding out of control, heading in our direction! Everyone began scrambling up the banking as there was nowhere else to go. Except me. I froze in place, staring at the vehicle heading straight for me, completely unable to move! Here I was, normally so brave and ready to take on most any obstacle... yet I froze! I can still remember trying to move my feet but they felt rooted to the spot. I couldn't understand what had come over me!

In less than a minute everyone was over the banking and screaming for me to move. With the car just a few yards away and coming fast, my friend Dana risked his life to help me. He slid back down, grabbed my arm and quickly dragged me forward as there was no time left to try and climb directly up. The out-of-control car then hit the exact spot where seconds earlier, I had stood immobilized, helplessly watching it speed directly toward me!

Dana was my Earth-Angel that day as he pulled me out of harm's way. He was fully present in the moment. He had no thought of how it would look or about being a hero. He was simply, fully in the moment, trusting his own Inner Wisdom, knowing that he could save me. I was awed, shaken, and immensely grateful.

Annoying Alarm Clock

While working in Houston I loved my 7am to 7pm schedule. The three days I had off one week, and the four the next, perfectly suited my lifestyle. I was able to 'live' at work and give my all to my patients for days in a row, and then shift my focus completely to fun and friends and exploring my life beyond work on my days off. It was great.

The hospital I worked for had three helicopters and a small jet. As you might imagine, we were very busy. There was no shortage of burn and trauma patients. Occasionally 12-hour shifts would turn into 14 hours or more which made for a very long day. One night, after working four extended shifts in a row, I found I was enormously relieved to finally head home. I had begun feeling tired back at the normal end of this last shift but had pushed through. I was content leaving my patients in the good hands of my fellow nurses. It felt so good to be a part of this team that made the welfare of our patients the number one priority. For this reason, some physicians would press hard to get their special patients admitted to our units. It was also, for this reason, that the other nurses and I would agree to push on and work the extra hours when Althea asked it of us. It was now very late, close to 10:30pm. I had been up and moving non-stop since waking up at 5:00 this morning. I was bone-tired.

The Houston police had a small substation located in our hospital because the crime in the city sometimes reached into the medical center and even at times into our hospital or parking garage.

I remember the usual police escort that walked me from the hospital through the parking garage to my car. I remember getting in to my car to drive home.

After that, the next thing I knew, I was hearing a noise far off in the distance. The noise persisted and gradually, so gradually, became louder and louder. Now it was becoming very annoying. It grew much louder, still persisting, and then so very loud. In that moment I realized I was asleep. It was like when you're sleeping and you hear your annoying alarm clock only faintly at first because you're so deeply asleep. It continues to ring and becomes louder and louder as you come up to the surface and finally it lifts you up out of the depths of sleep and wakes you. I opened my eyes, and found myself staring down at my lap! Puzzled, I lifted my head.

It took only a few seconds for my now rudely-awakened brain to fully comprehend what I was looking at. Once it registered, I saw to my complete horror, that I was not at home softly snuggled up in my bed, but out on the roadway driving my car! Not only that, I was traveling at a very high rate of speed and only a few car lengths ahead of me, a huge, hulking street sweeper was lazily making its way along the street directly in front of me! I couldn't believe it! I was completely shocked and horrified! Had I not woken up just when I did, I would have plowed right into the back of it! It was surreal!

After slamming on my brakes, and collecting myself, I turned to look out my driver's side window to find the source of the noise... the persistent sound that had woken me and saved my life.

Again, I was startled to see another car driving so close beside me. A man was looking over at me with his hand pressing hard on the horn in the center of his steering wheel. He had obviously noticed me with my head down and stayed along side of me, blaring his horn until he finally roused me. This was truly amazing since on weeknights at this time of night, there were generally very few, if any, other cars on this stretch of road. This complete stranger, my Earth Angel, had literally saved my life! Instantly, I realized the enormity of what he had done for me. I was flooded with gratitude. Unfortunately, I never got to thank him. Once he saw that I was ok, he waved and quickly sped off.

If not for this amazing soul, another Earth Angel who had been so completely present that he was able to notice me in my car with my head down, there would have been a terrible accident. My parents were saved a late-night phone call informing them that their only daughter, 23 years old, had died in a terrible car crash.

Musclebound Earth Angel

Many years later, I let a friend borrow my little Ford Ranger pickup truck. He returned to tell me that my gas tank was leaking a little when he put gas in it. This seemed crazy since it was fine when I had arrived in town earlier. I looked under the truck and there was no leaking now. It seemed okay so I decided to ask my brother Steve to check it out when I got back to Massachusetts.

Later in the day I was waiting outside by my truck for another friend and noticed that my tailgate wasn't shut all the way. I opened it and slammed it shut but it wouldn't close properly. This was strange as it always closed easily. I tried a few more times and still could not get it to close evenly. I was really perplexed.

Two couples were walking by at the time. One of the guys saw my struggle and offered to close it for me. After inspecting around it to be sure there was nothing in the way, he gave it first one, then another and then a really hard slam and finally closed it. I was so grateful! He just smiled and said he was glad he could help and walked off with his friends.

Soon after, I stopped for gas on my way out of town. I noticed some gas did leak out as I pumped it in so I stopped and called my brother Steve for advice about what to do. He thought a connection to the tank must have rusted through and suggested I get a funnel and a length of hose to get enough gas in so I could get back to Massachusetts where he would look at it.

I did as he suggested and headed out to the expansive highway to travel the two hours back to Massachusetts from New Hampshire.

It was a cold, clear, beautiful evening and my drive was uneventful. Darkness had set in by the time I arrived and Steve planned to look at the gas tank in the morning.

The next day, I was glad to hear that my gas tank was not rusted. However, I was shocked and horrified to hear that it was partially disconnected because directly behind my driver's door, the main frame of my truck was *completely broken in* half!

Steve was certain that closing the tailgate properly had straightened the truck bed and helped hold it together. This he believed gave stability to the frame and helped keep it from letting go completely as I was driving. Still, it was a long way to drive in such a fragile condition. Had it let go, the gas tank would have hit the highway and the sparks most likely would have caused it to explode. Not to mention that my truck would have broken apart on the highway! I was incredulous!

*Once again, a wonderful soul, an Earth Angel, had kept me safe on the roadway. This kind man was present and aware enough to notice my dilemma. His stopping and helping me close the tailgate had unknowingly saved my life!

As you might imagine, all of these experiences have greatly impacted my life and directed it much closer to connection with our Divine Source as well as to other people, animals, and nature.

At different times between these experiences that I have just shared with you, (and many, many others) I experienced two monumental events in my life that have had an even greater effect on me and my life, changing it in truly extraordinary ways. The following is the first of them:

Back to The Future

I had left Alaska months before to visit family and friends and to do some traveling. Now I had only just recently returned from a few months of visiting my close high school friend, Buffy, in Ecuador. My boyfriend Doug had joined me briefly to travel with a small group around the Galapagos Islands by boat.

By day we were enchanted with the islands and the wildlife on them. Lying on the deck at night, we had the once-in-a-lifetime experience of watching Haley's comet in all its glory. It would appear suddenly, seemingly out of nowhere, and cross the corner of the night sky, it's tail blazing behind it. In the clear, dark night sky, far away from any artificial light, it was a breathtaking, awe-inspiring sight!

At the end of our trip, Doug left to return to work while I traveled on to Miraflores and Cusco, Peru, and then on to explore Machu Pichu. After more traveling and exploring, including: a train ride to Riobamba (where I rode part of the way on the roof of the train with some other travelers!), a trip to the equator, and visits to the mountain village of Otovalo, I was now back in Massachusetts. I had met so many wonderful people on my journey and had so many wonderfully rich experiences.

I was visiting with family and friends in Massachusetts before moving on to Hawaii for a year or two. Life was magical! In my wildest dreams I never would have imagined that fate would step in and tip it so completely upside down:

It had been a perfect summer night. I had been leisurely driving home after a big all-day barbecue with close friends and family members at my parent's house. Then... that life-changing split second of fate stepped in:

Shortly before I got into my car to drive home, I had been given a 'message' intuitively that fate was about to step in to impact my life in a very big way. I remember lingering a while after everyone had gone home, going over the joys of the day with my mother, not yet ready to face whatever the Universe had in store for me. I could tell it would be truly life altering. I did not know how or when, but I 'felt' whatever was to be, would happen fairly soon.

The warm summer night was softly quiet and so perfect that I wanted to drink it all in as I drove home. Windows open, I drove peacefully along in my antique '56 Ford that I had lovingly restored with the help of my brother Steve and boyfriend Doug.

Although not mandatory at the time, the one task left was to install the seat belts that I had just purchased. Steve planned to do that the following weekend.

It was so beautiful out and I was so full of the wonderful day I had with everyone, that I was in no hurry to get home and go inside. Being nearly midnight, there were no other cars on this side road so I took my time. The night air filled the car like a soft, warm hug. I felt pleasantly relaxed yet not really tired.

Just as I began to enter the large, brightly lit, empty intersection, it was instantly alarming to suddenly notice a vehicle come speeding into it. It was running the red light! At first it did not fully compute when out of the corner of my eye I realized that it was headed straight for me! This, rather than straight out across the middle of the large intersection which was completely empty and where there was a wide expanse of space to avoid me. In that terrifying split second, I knew it was going to ram me at a very high rate of speed. With no time to move out of harm's way, I put my foot on the brake and clutched the steering wheel, bracing for the inevitable, literally holding on for dear life. Seconds before impact, I suddenly got the 'message' intuitively that I would not die. I relaxed.

Then it hit.

The impact was catastrophic for me. First there was the deafening sound of metal crushing metal; then the vague sensation of being slammed up against the door, my body violently hitting it, breaking the solid metal door handle in half. My head smacked against, and shattered the side window. I was being helplessly thrown around, back and forth and from one side of the car to the other like a crash test dummy. My head repeatedly slammed against the passenger door. It was dream-like. I was aware of the movements and impacts yet felt nothing. It seemed like it was all happening in some kind of floating dream cloud. Finally, it all ended in darkness.

My next awareness was of hearing what sounded like a group of teenagers anxiously talking about leaving. They sounded nearby as I heard them saying "Come on, we gotta get out of here! Leave the car! Let's go! Now! Let's go!" Another voice protested that they should not leave the accident scene - that they should wait.

I silently pleaded, "No, please don't leave me here like this. I need help." I tried to call out but I had no voice. Where was my voice? What was happening? I was so scared...then all was quiet.

They had left me!

I was abandoned and alone. It was then that I realized that I could not see! I don't know how long it took but I remember willing myself back from the depths until finally I was fully conscious and my vision returned. After a moment or so of disorientation - not understanding where I was - I discovered that I was wedged under the dashboard on the floor of the passenger side of my car with my feet tangled up where my clutch and brake pedals should be. As I went to lift my head, pain seared through it, overwhelming my senses and everything began to go black again. Immediately I lowered my head back to the floor. Then, after an unmeasurable period of time, I came back to consciousness and I could see again. Keeping my head on the floor, I attempted to free my feet. I couldn't see them or tell what shape they were in. I felt somewhat numb. I had no idea how badly injured I was but I knew I couldn't get up. The quiet was so empty and hollow. I was alone and helpless. Also, although I didn't know it at the time, I was in a state of shock.

I tried to slowly inch my head up to see why my feet would not come loose but the pain threatened to throw me back into unconsciousness again. I kept my head on the car floor wondering what to do, wondering what would happen from here.

After a period of time, my hope soared! I heard first one, then soon after, another car slow down, but my hope was crushed as I realized that they passed by. They did not stop! How could they simply drive by! Then I realized they could not see me. My car must just look like an empty wreck to them, the remnants of an earlier accident. What would happen to me? Would I be trapped here on the bare metal floor all night? I felt so helpless and unsure of what to do until I decided that one of them would surely report seeing my car and the police would arrive soon. In the meantime, I went to work focusing on first one foot, then the other, feeling my way, trying again to free them from the wreckage.

To her credit, the driver of the other car did not run off with her friends. She had stayed, quietly waiting for help to arrive. (No one had mobile phones at that time.) I imagine she was nearly as frightened as I was.

Perhaps because she was in a much larger, heavier old car, or perhaps because she was in a relaxed state from the alcohol, or maybe both, she was thankfully, relatively unharmed.

It was a very different scenario for me, however. That fate-filled night was the beginning of a journey through an entirely new existence for me. I spent the next several years severely restricted physically and in constant, unspeakable pain. I was told by one specialist after another that I had permanent damage and that I would never recover my previous state of health and independence. It seemed too big to be real.

After being on the car floor for what seemed like a very long time, feeling my way, I finally freed my feet. Then I heard the sirens. Help was coming!!!

It turned out that I had sustained a traumatic brain injury from a severe closed head injury. I had continual seizures, damage to joints and discs in my neck and back, a severe neck injury where nerves, tendons, ligaments and muscles in my neck were torn and damaged with some causing permanent nerve damage. Among other things, there was a fracture in my pubic bone and bruised ribs.

For a period immediately following the accident, I would sleep all night and much of the day. I ran low grade fevers from the massive inflammation throughout my body and slept and dozed throughout the days from exhaustion and the healing process. In the beginning, I could not fully articulate what I wanted to say. The words were in my head but for some reason I could not speak all of them. I could talk, I just could not get my brain to get my mouth to say all of the words I planned to say. This was terrifying! I couldn't understand what had happened. I remember trying hard not to panic. At the same time my terrified Mother kept telling me that I had no short-term memory. She kept trying to tell me things and I would have no memory of what she had just said minutes before. I also experienced angina initially. Later I was told I may have bruised my heart. Thankfully, these particular symptoms cleared rather quickly. However, for a while, due to my head injury and the extreme pain and fatigue, it was often hard to retain information or understand it clearly.

Surgery was continually encouraged for pain relief due to the damage of some of the discs in my neck and mid back. My jaw was knocked out of place and I could not open my mouth all the way. I had to have a device in place 24 hours a day and have regular orthodontic treatments for a year. My neck was locked up tight. I could not turn my head side to side or move it up and down. Periodically, a knife-like pain would suddenly slice through my ears with such a ferocious intensity, it would take my breath away. Then it would be gone. I developed severe fibromyalgia and later chronic fatigue syndrome as well.

Although I took medications for seizures, I still had some each day. These manifested as small blocks of 'missed time.' Meaning, I would be doing something, and then something else, and not even be aware that I had missed something in between. One of the most frightening examples was this:

One day, several years after the accident, I was preparing to take a bath. I put candles in a couple corners of the tub to create a more relaxing atmosphere. The tub was filled, the candles lit, and Doug was about to help me in. The next thing I knew, he was slapping my face hard between his hands. I was stunned! Before I realized what was going on,

I felt the pain of his open hands repeatedly hitting both sides of my face and my head, water being splashed in my eyes, and then the smell of burning hair. I had no idea what he was doing!

Unbeknownst to me, I had experienced another seizure and had leaned directly over one of the candles, my long hair falling into it. For that brief interval of the seizure, I was unaware that my hair was on fire. Doug had reacted quickly when he saw some of my hair go up in flames. Thankfully, the worst that came of it was that I forced into having my hair cut to even it out.

The trauma of the impact of the accident had caused all of the fascia (connective tissue) in my body to go into lock down. My physical therapist said she had never seen such a severe tightening of fascia, that it was the worst textbook case. As a result, I was incredibly restricted. Movement was intensely painful. I could not raise my arms very far from my body, turn my head side to side, or open my hands all the way, among other things. For a few years I was extremely hypersensitive to sound, touch, and temperature to the point where it would become so painful it would often bring me to tears. I had constant pressure and pain in my head as well as constant intense pain in my neck and back.

Part of the nerve damage stole my signal to know when I had to empty my bladder. So, for a period of time, I had to go and use the bathroom even though I felt no need to, otherwise my body would complain by creating terrible spasms when my bladder was too full. Brief activity and conversation were exhausting. I could sit or stand for short periods only. For several years I constantly had to get down and kneel on a pillow to take the pressure off and ease some of the additional pain that standing or sitting for the briefest periods would bring. I needed a wheelchair to go outside my home to appointments, etc. because walking more than a short distance was nearly impossible. Besides excruciating pain, I had foot drop (where the front of my foot hung down when I lifted it to take a step) This made it very difficult not to trip. Also, my right foot was lifted up sideways so I walked on the outside of that foot. For this reason, I had to wear a bulky brace to help hold my foot down flat. Gone were my cute sandals and high heels, even my sneakers. Now I had to wear clunky high tops with custom made orthotics inside and the brace on one side.

For the first few years, I had ice around my neck and down my spine nearly constantly from the time I woke up until the time I went to bed at night. Although I barely felt the cold in most areas, the ice temporarily helped numb the pain down to some degree. Medication was needed to sleep and even then I would wake up frequently during the night crying in pain. When I began to use a guided imagery recording, I was able to get to sleep easier and able to return to sleep more often when I woke up in the middle of the night like this. The guided imagery would direct me inside myself. After a short period of regular listening, a few times each day, it became a great temporary healing time-out.

For a long period of time I would regularly just doze off in the middle of eating. (I was not sedated) One minute I was carefully chewing some soft food, the next I was being rudely awakened by Doug or a family member. Like a small child, I was watched closely to prevent choking.

My time in the Rehabilitation hospital was scary. Most of the staff was professional, experienced, and dedicated. It was tough but they helped as much as they could.

The frightening part was the doctor in charge of my care. In my first meeting with him, I told him I had no idea how to live like this, so crippled and dependent. I told him I was spoiled by always enjoying good health, having freedom to work, travel and be creative. Now I was at a complete loss. He replied by asking me the definition of spoiled! I didn't understand the relevance. He went on to explain that spoiled meant rotten, like rotted fruit. What the heck? I was horrified! This frightened me. I told him I didn't feel that way, that maybe spoiled wasn't the best choice of words. I told him I needed to learn how to live as fully as I could in this condition until I was well. Again, I asked him if he could help me with that. He just stared at me for a few uncomfortable moments and then very dryly said," No one has ever asked that question before."

In that moment I wondered just what kind of place I was in! Didn't people come here to get their life back as best they could? Wouldn't everyone want to get the absolute most from being there?

In my second encounter with him, he told me I could no longer use ice to help numb the pain. He offered no other option.

Again, I was horrified! He was taking away one of the few tools I had to help ease some of the constant, nearly unbearable pain I experienced. He went on to tell me that it was for my own good, otherwise I would become addicted to it. Addicted to icing! Was this man really a physician? Was he sane? This was so frightening! When he left my room, I just cried, not knowing how I would survive my time in this terrible place. Doug was still away in Florida and I felt terribly weak and alone. I felt I was at the mercy of this incompetent man.

It just so happened that my door was open and another patient passing by saw me crying and stopped to ask what was wrong. I explained to him and he cursed the doctor. "Everyone knows he's a cruel, crazy, bas----! He stops everyone from using ice that benefits from it! Then just this morning he had the poor lady in 203 in tears. She has MS and came in because it has progressed to where she needs to use a wheelchair. He told her that it was her own doing! That if she tried harder, she could walk! He's nuts! I see her in PT. She tries harder than most of us in here and doesn't give up! Even her husband says she's always been a fighter, always pushing to do better! Everyone that knows her is really upset. Her husband just came in and he wants to take her out of here and go somewhere else! So don't listen to him. I'll get the ice for you. We all sneak it. He never knows."

From that point on I was able to continue icing my spine and neck thanks to this kind stranger. - (and no one was happier than me when years later, I no longer needed to!)

The third experience I had with the doctor was one day when I really thought I might be dying. I genuinely felt like I might stop breathing. I had no idea why. My chest felt so heavy it felt leaden. It was an effort to inhale. I could barely move. I could barely talk. I couldn't call for help. I had this horrible growing feeling of impending doom. It felt like my brain and body were shutting down. I didn't understand why it was happening and I was terrified. As I lay on my bed focusing on the now tremendous effort it was to inhale, I looked over at the beautiful gift basket that my dear, sweet friend, Valerie Boyes had made for me. It was full of candy and chocolates. It had been sitting there awhile since I had no desire for sweets and had little interest in food in general since the accident. However, in that moment I was drawn to take out a couple of Hershey's Kisses. I really didn't feel like eating them. Actually, the thought of it was repulsive to me at that time.

It was also a tremendous effort to reach them but I was being very strongly nudged by my Divine guidance to do so.

So, I did. Minutes after eating one, my feeling of doom lifted and I felt much brighter. After the second one the heaviness lifted and I felt I could breathe again! Even though I had never had an experience like this before, I now realized that my blood sugar must have been dangerously low. (I am not diabetic.) Valerie's chocolate appeared to have saved me from going into a hypoglycemic coma! The thought of it gave me chills!

About 10 minutes later the doctor happened to come by. I told him what I had just experienced. He responded by saying, "Well, I guess the lesson for today is that you should always carry around a couple of Hershey's Kisses in your pocket. It's ok to do that you know." Then he turned and left.

God help me! Have I survived this horrible accident to die at the hands of this incompetent impostor of a doctor? Again, I felt helpless and alone. Doug was still in Florida. (He would not return until I was being discharged.)

Miraculously, however, I did survive and I did get to finally go home to continue PT (physical therapy) and my other therapies as an outpatient for many years at a different location.

I know this was only possible because another doctor was soon assigned to my case. Tonie Moran, PhD, was one of the psychologists who saw patients as part of the rehab program. I felt she was a true gift from the Divine. In my first meeting with her I at once felt safe and cared for. Being so weak and vulnerable from extensive injuries, I now knew I had a caring, competent professional looking out for my wellbeing. I could rest easier and focus on my rehabilitation without worrying about what other bizarre, and potentially harmful thing the other doctor might, or might not, do.

Dr. Moran was adept at understanding the enormous impact that major trauma has on your whole being. More importantly, however, she knew just how to help me deal with living in a pain-filled crippled body and the dramatically reduced life I had been suddenly thrust into. She helped me find a place in it.

At the same time, she helped me stay focused on the excruciatingly painful, minuscule steps forward, encouraging and supporting me along the way. She remained an expert source of support and guidance for years after I left the Rehab. I am forever grateful to her for her wise, patient, compassionate healing. She has been a major blessing in my life.

 After the fifth year into my recovery, Doug and I moved into a handicapped apartment and the building had a heated pool. Doug wanted to stay living with my parents because it was cheaper and he worried about my being alone without family there but I could easily afford it at the time and I needed some semblance of independence back. Also, I was still needing a lot of quiet time to rest. I would doze off and on during the day and easily tire after any therapy or minor physical or mental exertion. Just the sound of the TV was painful.

Each evening I would ask him to bring me down to the pool in the wheelchair and we would both go in. Putting on my bathing suit was impossibly difficult but I was determined. My brother Marty had bought me a special flotation belt and I could move around the pool gently and easily with it while Doug swam. The water was very healing and I was determined to get well. The belt supported me and the water refreshed and renewed me. My strength slowly, finally, began returning to where I could walk part of the short distance back to the elevator.

At this point I was still having PT three times a week and cranio-sacral therapy once a week. PT was still a torturous process for me but I knew it was necessary. Riding in the car was pure hell until my brother Steve found me a car in which the passenger seat electronically reclined nearly flat. This prevented the excruciating pull of inertia inside my head as the car was moving. It was so awful. I remember fantasizing about being magically transported back and forth to PT by helicopter so I wouldn't have to take that horrible ride in the car. Until I got the other car, it seemed that the tortuous ride home would negate all the good PT had done that day.

It was my Uncle Robert who so lovingly devoted his time to take me to these appointments three days a week, week

after week, month after month, year after year until he died. He was devastated over my condition and prayed daily for my complete recovery. He was there for support and sat with me with no need to talk or be entertained. He was comfortable in the silence which was a great gift to me. He recognized that since the accident, idle conversation drained me. It was like painful, grating noise. So, we would frequently ride to and from PT with few words spoken. Just having him there with me felt comforting, loving and safe. I am forever grateful for having him in my life. He had always been my best friend and confidant growing up. I loved him dearly. His unrelenting love helped me keep going.
Later, finding him dead one morning was devastating.

At some point along the way it was suggested that I try some gentle chiropractic treatment. I was referred to a man in Concord, MA.

I went a couple of times and found it was mild enough to tolerate. The ride back and forth however, was painful and exhausting but I was determined to do whatever I could to help my healing.

On one visit he gave me a patient gown and asked me to remove my top and bra so he could better evaluate my spine. My head was fogged with pain and exhaustion, plus the brain injury had numbed or slowed much of my cognitive faculties so I didn't even think to question it. When he stepped out, I changed.

When I stood to get ready to get dressed, instead of leaving the room again, he quickly came around behind me and slipped his sweaty little hands under my patient gown. He grabbed my breasts and began squeezing them obscenely with those disgustingly foul feeling things! I was so shocked that I couldn't even move at first. I couldn't even speak! I just couldn't believe this was happening! Thoughts moved in slow motion and then I was able to start to move away. With this, he quickly left the room. Now the full impact of what had transpired made its way through the stupor of my poor injured brain. I was horrified! Here I was so weak and vulnerable and this horrid little man, a health care professional who was supposed to be safe and intent on assisting with my healing, had taken advantage of me! - of his patient!! I felt soiled and disgusted.

Driving home with my mother I was in a state of shock and repulsion. I couldn't speak about it because I was so humiliated, grossed out, and still processing it. Later, my mother wondered why I refused to go to any more appointments there. I just couldn't speak of it to her or anyone. Dealing with being so weak and defenseless was difficult enough without having to deal with this unthinkable, perverted assault. I just had to put it away somewhere and go on...or so I thought.

Soon after this, however, I developed a real fear of being alone whenever I was outside of our apartment. It felt crazy. I knew I had no real reason to be afraid like this but I couldn't shake it. I have always been one to face fears head on and push through them. Now, if I found myself waiting in the car for a few minutes while Doug or a family member who drove me ran into the drugstore or bank, I felt a terrible fear rise up in me. It really upset me because I had no idea where it was coming from. It would quickly grow so ominous that I would be compelled to lock myself in until whoever was driving me came back to the car.

I would try to stay alert enough to quickly hit the unlock button on my door when I saw them coming so they wouldn't know. Too often, however, I would quickly doze off and then be jarred awake by "Hey" and a few raps on the window. I felt ridiculous.

One evening I was resting on my bed in my parent's house. The room was darkened and Doug snuck in, not wanting to disturb me. As he walked in and neared my side of the bed, I suddenly became aware of someone there and instinctively grabbed a pair of scissors off the nightstand, slashing out, as best I could, hoping to protect myself. Thankfully I did not reach him but as you might imagine he was shocked. Now I knew I really needed help releasing this fear. Fortunately, I had Dr. Moran to help me. Working together, I was able to release it completely. What a relief!

Over the years I occasionally refused to go to a PT appointment and would cancel. It didn't happen often but periodically I needed to give myself a time-out from it all. I knew I needed to go to do my part to become well again.

Also, I couldn't bear to let my uncle, or later my father down. So I would begin again with my very next appointment.

As tough as PT was, I realized early on how very blessed I was to have Mary Cronin as my physical therapist. I don't recall who recommended her but she is definitely a rare gift. Not only is she a highly gifted PT, she is a beautiful, unassuming, compassionate woman who gives 120% to her patients. Everyone I have recommended her to over the years has thanked me. They love her. She glows with a beautiful radiance that you can feel coming through you when she works on you. She helped inch me forward through the pain and restriction of the injuries. She understood the times when I could not hold back tears. She was always there offering comforting words while never giving up on me, despite the extent of my injuries. For eight long years we persevered together. Through the tears and the milestones, she was there for me and I am forever grateful for her care and unwavering support. I am also honored to now call her my friend.

The many doctors and specialists that I saw over the years all agreed that I would never fully recover and would be incapacitated for the rest of my life. I hated seeing them because of their discouraging words. I didn't want to hear it and I never believed them. My Divine intuition had assured me that I would get my life back. Even though my nursing experience agreed with the diagnosis and damage assessment, I still 'knew' I would recover. I can't tell you exactly how it was conveyed to me but when I stepped away from the fear and stayed unassuming and open to all possibilities, these clear 'knowings' would suddenly enter my thoughts. They were never wrong. I just 'knew' I would have a miracle and get my life back. I chose to trust. This upset Doug tremendously as he had little confidence in my 'Divine messages' and thought I was deceiving myself. He didn't trust in my gift of 'knowing.' He was a constant witness to my terrible, crippled up life style. Over the years he saw my many futile attempts to push forward, knowing that I was not ready yet. At home, he alone witnessed the excruciating pain, and the reduced version of the woman I had once been. So many times he had to try and talk me out of pushing harder and further, knowing I was not capable and could easily hurt myself, which at times, I did... So badly did I want to be back to 'normal.'

As torturous as it was to ride in the car to go back and forth to therapy week after week, year after year, I continued. I didn't hope, I didn't think about when, I just 'knew' I would have my life back.

One day my dear friend Joan suggested I see this woman Judith Swack of 'Healing from the Body Level Up'. Judith, a PhD and practicing scientist, visionary, teacher and healer, uses her unique system of mind/body healing techniques to release stress and trauma, allowing the body, mind, and spirit to regain balance. Joan believed that Judith could help me heal from the debilitating pain and multiple injuries I had incurred in the accident. Although I didn't fully understand it at the time, I decided to give her a try. That decision proved to be a pivotal one, because in an indirect way, she did just that.

I felt an immediate connection with Judith. When I called to make my first appointment, I asked her receptionist Marcia, a lovely, kindhearted person, to explain Judith's technique to me. Then Judith got on the phone herself. When she began speaking to me, I suddenly felt this powerful bolt of energy shoot from me to her and from her to me at the same time. It took me so by surprise! Before I could begin to wonder what had just happened, I was shocked again when Judith immediately said "Did you feel that? You felt that, didn't you?" She had experienced the same thing! At once I knew that I needed to meet with her and we met for a few individual sessions. They were unlike anything I had ever imagined or heard of. During each one I would feel energy shifts in my body and have some sort of incredibly unique experience with energies from other realms. One day she told me she was getting a very strong intuitive 'message' that I needed to attend a workshop that would be held in her meeting room. She said I could lie down in the next room as much as I needed and they would give me energy flushes to help me get through as well. She insisted that I really needed to be there. It sounded completely crazy given the condition I was in, but when I asked my inner guidance, I knew intuitively that she was right, that I did need to attend.

Since I still had chronic fatigue from the head injury as well as debilitating pain and restriction each day, I wondered how I would make it through even the first few hours. Doug was certain I wouldn't and he was very much against my attending. However, I was determined, 'knowing' that I was meant to be there. Finally, he relented and agreed to get me there and back. Each day was an enormous struggle. I would be so wiped out when he picked me up that I would go directly to bed when we arrived home, barely brushing my teeth, skipping dinner and once falling asleep in my clothes. The alarm clock would surprise me the next morning as it seemed impossible that the night had passed so quickly.

Doug was deeply concerned that I was overdoing it. Unhappy as he was, thankfully, he continued to drive me.

Although painful and exhausting, it was wonderful to be out and be part of a social group again. There was little talking but I fed on the contact. There were only around a dozen of us and everyone was very nice and never made issue over my condition or my need to have help with getting through the day.

Then, one day, eight years after the accident, three days into the workshop, I had an experience that transformed my life.

Actually, it gave me my life back.

We were all sitting, listening to the instructor lecture. She was drawing a stick figure on the board and describing how your energy field can be affected in times of shock and trauma. It was interesting but I was having trouble staying focused as I was fading out from fatigue and pain. I so badly wanted to get up and go into the other room to lie down for a bit. However, that would take having to cross in front of everyone to do so. I knew we were just about to take a break so I was trying to hold out.

I was sitting in my chair, the last in the row, furthest from the instructor. As I was struggling to get into a better place with my physical state, no longer able to stay focused on her teaching, out of the blue a vibration began below my feet. Initially I thought it was something going on with the building, like the furnace or something, but that thought passed quickly as the vibration began to travel up through the bottoms of my feet. Now I could feel the power of it. Incredibly, it somehow seemed as though it originated in the center of the earth! It continued up my legs and as it climbed higher, it increased in intensity. It was now incredibly strong in my legs, to the point where they began to shake. I wondered what was going on! I looked over at the others and they seemed completely unaware as they were all sitting quietly listening to the instructor. Now it was traveling up my body. My legs were shaking harder and my body was trembling. Soon my knees were knocking together. It climbed through my body and suddenly bright red blood burst into my vision from the left side and continued across my line of vision! Then, just as suddenly,

I had the sensation of being covered in blood. It was on my clothing and my hands, and I could even feel it warm and wet on the back of my neck. Now, shaking uncontrollably from the energy, I instinctively began wiping my hands on my pants, trying to wipe off the very distinct feeling of blood, at the same time knowing that I could not. I was feeling a bit panicky at this point. Looking over at the others, I could see that they were unaffected and still had no idea what was happening to me. They were all focused on the instructor. Meanwhile, the blood felt warm and sticky on my hands but I could not wipe it off. I realized that I was somehow experiencing two dimensions simultaneously but I had no idea how or why. The vibration had become so intense throughout me that my teeth began to chatter. Break was then called and everyone got up to leave the room. I prepared for their shock when they saw me but they were all ahead of me and preoccupied as I slowly moved into the lady's room to furiously wash my hands. Still, the very real feeling of the blood remained so I went to the instructor for help. One look at me and she knew something was up. I was obviously distressed as my teeth were chattering and I was shaking very hard all over. She asked if I would like to have her work with me privately or let the class watch. I didn't care. I just knew I needed some help. The intensity of the energy was incredible! Immediately she called the class back and gave them the choice of going in the other room and practicing the last lesson as planned, or staying and observing a healing that I had volunteered for. Knees knocking, teeth chattering, and my body shaking furiously all over, I sat where I was directed. She sat close by across from me, and as part of the class looked on, asked me to close my eyes and go to the source of the experience. Instantly I went fully into another time and place! Here, I was looking at a horrific site with horrible carnage of thousands of people. There was blood and death and dying everywhere I looked! It was a slaughter of what seemed like colossal proportions and I was immediately shocked and overwhelmed. As I began crying, the instructor's voice suggested I step back and move away to a more comfortable place. I did as instructed and found myself off to the side, somewhat separated, like an observer. Here I was up on small knoll nearby. This bloody massacre had taken place on beautiful, bright green rolling hills with dense forest on either side. I was looking out over the thousands of dead and wounded down to my right. I was beyond horrified and intensely sad. People were screaming and moaning and wailing in agony and loss. It was awful! In front of me was a man dressed in a brown shirt and pants. He had longish brown hair and I noticed he was left-handed. (Later I would be told that during the experience I was using only my left hand to accept tissues to wipe my eyes. This is something I would normally use my right hand for and I am not ambidextrous.) He was kneeling in the grass tending to a badly wounded person. His hands and clothing were covered in blood. I could see that he had fresh blood on his neck as well, even though he wasn't bleeding. In this moment, I knew he was a healer and that he was feeling very overwhelmed and shocked himself. I then realized; he was me! I was stunned! Here I was looking at myself as a male healer in this other realm.

My instructor continued to guide me through healing in this space. When we were finished, I 'returned' fully to this existence, back to the room. Once I was fully aware of myself and my surroundings, I felt light and bright as sunshine. Where I had been crying nearly nonstop throughout the whole unimaginable experience, I was now filled with unbounded joy and began laughing simply from an abundance of the pure joy that had become me. My body was light with joy and laughter. I realized something had radically changed - it was me! I was completely well! As soon as I realized this, I jumped up from my chair and began waving my arms and dancing around, laughing all the while. I had not been able to move my arms more than 1/2 way up to shoulder height for eight years! Now I could wave them around over my head! I could jump and dance and move my whole body freely!!! So freely!!! I had actually forgotten how that felt! It was like I was feeling certain muscles move in certain ways for the very first time ever! Where my whole body had been bound down by pain, inflammation, and tightened fascia, it now had total freedom! There was no restriction or pain anywhere with any movement. I was bursting with an energy that was pure joy and a clarity that seemed almost other-worldly. It felt Heaven sent - and I knew it was! It was also contagious. It seemed to fill the room and everyone in it. Now we were all laughing joyously together. There was no bit of anxiety or self-consciousness in the room. All were joy filled!

Moments later Doug arrived to pick me up. He stopped short in the doorway when he saw me. He didn't enter the room. The instructor beckoned him in, but he hesitated.

I called out to him, "Doug I'm back! I'm Back!"

He said, "What's going on? What have you done with Sharon?"

The instructor joyfully replied, "She's right here! She's back! Isn't it wonderful?"

He said, "She looks like Sharon and sounds like Sharon but that's not Sharon. What have you done with my girlfriend?"

I said, "It's me Doug! I'm back! I'm Back!' It's wonderful! I'm Back!" I jumped up and down some more, waving my arms around as I called to him.

The instructor joyfully said again, "Isn't it great!" and everyone was smiling and laughing while agreeing and welcoming him in. Finally, he very tentatively came in and guardedly joined the celebration in spite of himself. I was filled with an incredibly light, joyful laughter and laughed all the way home. This was still contagious, because as much as Doug wanted to be serious and get answers, he became filled as well and we both laughed together the entire 30 minutes or so that it took to get home!

The next day I was aware that I was no longer having seizures! So I cut down on my medication to test it and was able to stop it the next day. I have never had another seizure. I felt supercharged for weeks. Not hyper, just unbelievably wonderful. Not high, but like I could almost walk on air, as if I was made of pure Divine love...as I am, as we all are. All of my senses were beautifully heightened. It was as if my body was working at its absolutely fullest potential. Now completely unencumbered, I sang and jumped and danced around our apartment, glowing, beaming, I was so joyful! I delighted in moving my body! I was set free from the straight jacket of pain and injuries that had held my body imprisoned for so many days, so many years of my life! To say I was immensely grateful and overjoyed at being given this gift to fully re-enter life again is far beyond an understatement!

Sadly, during this time, rather than being thrilled that I was back, Doug was unable to rejoice with me. He remained focused on believing that I was under some sort of hypnosis and would soon revert back to my previous condition.

Greatly removed from the outside world, I had lived much of the past eight years as a shut-in. Everyday simple activities such as washing up, getting dressed, constant icing, and PT stretches used up most of my energy the first six years. Appointments and treatments stole the rest. In between, I rested and slept and used and reused my visualization recordings. I had little interest in the outside world the first six years as I was dulled out, easily exhausted, and focused on surviving the pain. Occasionally Doug took me to my parent's home for a brief visit. In later years, one of them or a friend would take me to a store or to the mall in the wheelchair. Sadly, I experienced sensory overload very quickly. Exhausted, I returned home disappointed and needing to lie down. Then, the last two years, as I gained strength and had short periods where the pain was tolerable, I began to have brief times out each week. Still, my life was a fraction of what it had once been.

Now I stepped back into life as a healthy, vibrant woman with greatly enhanced senses. I could 'see' and move with greater ease beyond our usual limited boundaries. Looking at someone now with my 'other sight', I could 'see' the cause of their fear and how to untangle it. Beautiful colors surrounded people. I would 'send' healing energy to them in any color and watch as it appeared around them. Energy flowed out of the palms of my hands.

Besides that, I felt like Rip Van Winkle as I stepped back into the world after nearly a decade had passed. Things had happened in the world, some friends had married and relocated. New music, new books, and new restaurants abounded. Some friends and family members had new relationships, new interests and changed lifestyles. For me, however, life seemed to begin again right where I had left off. Except now I was changed. I felt a deep sense of inner peace and connection that I previously felt during meditation. Now it lived in me. I felt like a much-enhanced version of my true self with a much greater sense of connection to the Divine.

It was so pleasant simply being. All of life was as it was meant to be. In a way I had stepped out of the past and into the future, even as many of my life memories stemmed from eight years ago. People who hadn't seen me for a while marveled at how young I looked. Time seemed to have stood still for me all those years.

There was a lot of catching up to do!

The 2nd of what I consider the two most monumental life changing events in my life so far, is as follows....

Becoming Heaven

My husband Kevin passed on a few years ago. We had thoroughly enjoyed one another and had such a delightful time together. We would laugh and love and play and have wonderful, deep philosophical discussions together. We both loved meeting new people, enjoying time with family and friends, and spending time in nature.

Kevin was a popular comedian who loved performing and loved his fans. At the time I was an RN working as a life enhancement guide and an end-of-life consultant.

We were enjoying our life together... then one day cancer thrust itself into it. Long before Kevin and I met, he had dealt with Melanoma. Now it had returned. This time it was throughout his entire system. With no known conventional cure, Kevin was given only 3 - 6 months to live... If he had his leg amputated and several lymph nodes removed, along with radiation and immune therapy. All of this even though there was no chance for a cure.

Life as we knew it was forever changed.

He was continually urged to have his leg cut off and to have these treatments in the hopes they would give him an extra month or two, no more. He declined. He told the doctor that he did not want to spend the last few months of his life without his leg. He also did not want to spend them recovering from surgery or going back and forth to doctor appointments and treatments. He wanted to have use of both legs and live as fully as he could for as long as he could, enjoying being at home and doing comedy... not in a hospital or treatment center. So, we decided to ride the fear together and do the best we could to continue to live our lives in whatever time we had. We continued to live our life together, but now we were three...Cancer, Kevin and me.

Even as the cancer hung on, Kevin became vibrantly healthy and looked and felt years younger following a holistic plan from the Hippocrates Health Inst. that I set up and managed for him. Although living with his diagnosis was a major life change for both of us, we lived most of our days with joy and gratitude, feeling deeply in love. We were also blessed with the love and good wishes of many people. Our families and friends, and thousands of his fans, rallied behind him. Privately we had a small group of loving, dedicated friends and family members that knew how altered our life had become. They knew how precious each new day was and that soon we would run out of them. We could speak honestly and openly together. They stood beside us through our ups and downs and stayed quietly nearby throughout our journey. They were the only ones that knew about:

*The Fear,

*The tremendous work it now often took for Kevin to maintain a semblance of a normal lifestyle.

*The many times that Kevin began to fail and I gently helped him back.

*The loss I initially felt from missed time with friends and from my work.

 *The loss we both felt from losing our carefree lifestyles and any promise of a future here together.

Sadly, I also lost many of my loved ones along the way. At the very start, while Kevin and I were still dealing with the impact of his diagnosis, the first three of my long-time friends passed on.

Before l would say goodbye to Kevin here in this realm, too many of my treasured friends would be gone from this life as well. It was a very challenging time for me. Life and death continued on around us. Still, we focused on the many joys and felt deep gratitude for them.

Then the day arrived when I was told by intuitive message that it was time...that Kevin's end here was near. I wanted to pretend it wasn't so but I knew full well that it was. Early on I had been 'told' that Kevin and I would have only a short time here together... That he would be continuing his journey 'there', as I would be here and that we would remain connected, always. I cried out my sorrow over his upcoming departure from this precious life we shared together. Then I took some deep breaths and centered myself for the final phase of our journey here together. I won't pretend that it was always easy. Besides the deaths of so many dear friends, there were a number of times over the years that Kevin would begin to falter. His health would begin to decline and he would feel like he was beginning to slip away. During these times he would fall into fear and I would sit and ask my Inner Wisdom for guidance. Each time I would receive a very clear intuitive 'message' about what to do next. Each time Kevin would trust and do whatever it was to regain his vibrant health. I just continued to trust in our Divine wisdom and accept our destiny.

Soon after receiving the 'message' that it was time for Kevin to pass on, he did. It was nearly six years after the reoccurrence of the disease.

One day, weeks after he had passed, I was sitting on our couch thinking about how I really should get up and dig out the papers the lawyers had asked me for over a week earlier. However, I was still feeling completely exhausted from being up night and day with Kevin during the last two months of his life. I really needed a bit of time to catch up. It seemed that such a big part of me had been torn away with him. I felt empty to my core. I was so exhausted I couldn't even sleep at night so I decided to put the task off another day and just sit.

As I was sitting there, gazing out at the blue sky and endless ocean, I experienced what most would describe as a near death experience. I 'visited' Heaven and Kevin. The difference was that I was not dying or ill, I just went into this expanded experience while sitting on the couch in my living room. I cannot tell you exactly how or why at this time. No matter. - I am forever changed.

I have been an RN in ICU, Trauma and Adult Burns. I have also worked in Hospice and then as an end-of-life consultant and guide. From an early age I 'knew' that people were needlessly frightened of death. People often comment that it takes a special person to be with someone as they pass from this life. I try to explain that it is only fear, covered by a great sense of loss that blocks the beauty of the 'end' of life process. It is I and others who attend the dying that are given the greatest gift each time we accompany someone through each precious last moment of life here in this physical world. To me, death has the same energy as birth. Each time I witness the incredible transformation of one phase of life to the next, I feel honored and humbled.

Feeling completely empty that day, I sat looking out at the ocean. Suddenly a 'portal' or opening appeared in the air just off to the left in the open space in our living room. I turned and looked in and was at once filled with overwhelming unconditional love and unbounded joy as I looked into Heaven! I did not physically leave the couch. I simply looked in. At once I saw Kevin and watched as he was walking along, happy and at ease. At the same time, I saw his entire life play out, seeing it all at once, as well as one event at a time. I saw individual events and his whole lifeline all at the same time.

Then I was transported.

Bodiless.

Dissolved into the ALL.

Immersed in, and part of, radiating *Magnificence.*

Where I had been deeply grieving Kevin's physical separation from me prior to this experience, here there was no separation. All was One. I was One with Kevin as he was with me and with the Divine and with All. Separation did not exist. Therefore, there was no feeling of loss... so no capacity for grief. Even as we maintained our individual uniqueness, Kevin was in me and of me as I was of him and of All. He 'lived' in me as I 'lived' in him as the Divine lives in us all. Here I 'got' it. I understood. Here there was no judgment, no separation, no suffering, no comparison, no needs; not even a thought about any of this. All was One with complete, delightfully loving perfection. All alive as a whole in vibrant, live *Magnificence.*

Previously, when I have 'crossed thresholds' and met with loved ones that have passed, I have been eager to embrace them and felt so joyful to be doing so. I saw them as I knew them in the physical (only they were now completely peaceful, joy filled, love filled and youthful). I can now see this was because there was still some level of separation that existed. 'Here' there was none. There was no containment of the physical so no need for embrace. This desire no longer existed in me because of being One with Kevin and One with All. Embracing him lived within me and I was the embrace. He was the embrace. The Divine was the embrace, as were all others. Everything and everyone. Perfect love. All Encompassing *Magnificence!*

This was a much fuller, complete experience. I was full of his love, my love, Divine love, all love. All melded together yet able to recognize Kevin's essence and he mine. Not a 'high'. The same delightful, loving fullness that I feel for Kevin (magnified), I now felt for All... no longer greater love for Kevin than for others. Love was equal, complete and magnified beyond the greatest imagination.

'Here' I got it. I could see through the simple falseness of judgment and fear - Always to the love.

I was complete with a fullness I could not have imagined before. All was delightfully as it was meant to be. No thoughts as we know them, just a lovely brilliance that contained all. No ecstasy or bliss. No overwhelming feelings. Just pure, radiant, endless *Magnificence.* Divine Brilliance. No needs. No concerns. Just all-encompassing vibrant Love. Pure, Shimmering, Brilliant, Divine love.

Although I experienced this as a separate 'place' initially by seeing the 'Portal', it then became a living state for me. I now know that 'Heaven' is everywhere we allow it. It is all the same event.

The first time and each time thereafter when I 'visited' through the 'portal' over the next few weeks I returned with the experience that the upper half of the trunk of my body was as it normally is, yet at the same time, that part of my solid body had dissolved into pure, highly vibrating essence. It was a beautiful, sparkling, vibrating, non-solid space. I went through my days with this, being solid yet not.

For a while after, when I thought about those that I had avoided or disliked or judged in some way, I could clearly see the falseness of it and could feel only the same degree of love for them, as for Kevin. We truly are all One with the other and with the Divine. I still feel this when I am fully present.

I am forever changed.

I can never un-know.

I have been pulled back some by life circumstances but I can never un-know. Often, I feel love swell up in me like a tidal wave that washes through each tiny cell of my being for the tiniest flower, a blue sky, a warm breeze, or when seeing a friend or stranger...etc., etc., etc.! It overpowers any fears or defenses and as I dissolve into it, it lovingly reminds me of who we truly are!

Afterward

As I stated in the beginning, my purpose in sharing some of my life experiences with you has been to offer you a greater sense of hope and sense of purpose, as well as opening you up to considering unlimited possibilities. I trust that you now have a greater understanding of how a regular, simple practice of pausing, going within, and learning to listen to your inner guidance will begin to enhance your life and the lives of those around you.

My wish for you is that you begin to trust your Intuition, your Inner Wisdom, the Divine Power that lives inside of you, inside each of us...that Divine Light that _is_ you... and All.

In the grand scheme of things, I am just an ordinary woman. I don't have super powers. I simply choose to remind myself that I am Divine at my core - as we all are, and take time to be in silence each day. Also, I continue to be dedicated to my spiritual practice of noticing and releasing control and judgment, living with kindness, living in the moment, and allowing and trusting whatever I am given.

This life has many joys and many challenges. I have ups and downs like everyone else. Being human, I still have times when I slip and fall into fear or victimhood. However, this happens much less now and when I stay connected to my center, the 'downs' no longer feel bad. They are just 'what is' and I look at the message they offer.

If I begin to feel drained and if I don't stop and take care, this can lead to being caught up in, and overwhelmed by, the fear and uncertainty of the ego. My focus can get pulled away from my center and out into the world's drama. I can fall into thinking like a victim or feeling hurt or jealous or sad or angry, or feeling the need to control some part of my life. Then I realize what I'm allowing and go back to my practice…remembering my Divine core… back to stopping and noticing what I feel in my body and allowing it, even when it feels very intense. Allowing it to finally move through leaves me centered and at peace once again. I'm not hiding from, or blocking out the world around me, just simply moving through it with more inner peace and happiness. I am more able to calmly respond to drama, anger, fear, and chaos. Now I can more easily see when I am triggered and react out of fear, anger (fear), or judgement (fear), and reach to my practice to heal that fear.

All kinds of wonderful things occur when I am centered in the present moment. I see the beauty in everything and everyone around me. It fills me with such love and joy and gratitude! I go through my days with a delightful glow inside.

In our fast-paced world many of us are programed to go along with the crowd. Instead, stop and take time to be quiet. Begin to pay attention to where your thoughts are.

Notice how things feel to you. Make your own choices. Stand strong. Start simple. Notice where you get caught up in judgment or negative thoughts. Notice where you feel you need to be right and where you try to control. Choose to let go and live with kindness... both for yourself and others.

It doesn't have to be perfect, just begin.
It does not matter how old you are, what color you are, or how you look or feel. It does not matter where you grew up, what happened in your past, who you choose to love, or what anyone else thinks or says about you. It does not matter what you've been told, or what you believed. Now you *know* that the Divine Light shines within you... Always. That Divine Light that *is* you. And everyone and everything.

Begin to take time each day to get quiet. If inner peace, happiness, and connection with the Divine are important to you, make time for your practice. Set a new schedule for yourself. Decide in what ways you want to begin to live differently and write it down. Leave yourself reminders. Pay attention to your thoughts and words and feelings. Notice where you judge and why. Judgment of anything or anyone comes from fear. So notice all the big and little places where you judge and commit to looking at that fear and replacing it with love and kindness. Stop and feel it in your body and allow it to move through you. Get assistance with this when you need it.

Always take care and be kind to yourself.

Spend time with those that respect themselves and others. Don't let bullies, or negative, or victim-minded folks drag you down. You no longer have to listen to them. Stop now! Send out a prayer for them. Then, seek out those that are supportive of the precious spark of Divine that makes you uniquely you. Spend time with them.

Turn inward and begin to listen to your heart, to your Divine self. You have full permission from the Highest Power to do this!

Spend time in Nature. Live in the moment. Return to it each time you get caught up with thoughts of the past or the future.

One way to help break the cycle of negative and fearful thoughts is by chanting or singing or listening to music. Have it ready for when you need it. Chanting or singing breaks the negative train of thought. Find something comforting or fun. Play the song (in your head or out loud) whenever you find yourself getting caught off center (as long as you are not driving or engaged in another activity that requires your full attention). Play it and listen to it until your mood shifts. Then commit to exploring that fear with someone helpful or when you have the quiet time to do so. It has been my experience, especially in the beginning, that it is much easier to move through different fears with someone or a group that is helpful at dealing with this.

Reach out when you need to. We are all sharing this planet and this life here together. It's a wonderful time to be alive! Enjoy the journey!

With love and best wishes for you,
Sharon

"Life is about Love, and we are Already Home."

Acknowledgements

I'd like to send out a special thanks to two wonderful best-selling authors;

Roland Merullo took time out to offer me valuable advice. I believe much of his writing is a great gift to anyone on their spiritual path. He offers deep life lessons and metaphors for spiritual growth throughout many of his unique stories. He has the ability to create fun, entertaining stories that show us how we judge ourselves and others, and reminds us to be better human beings. It is a pleasure to read his books. I especially enjoy 'Golfing With God' and 'American Savior'.

An equally special thanks to Penney Peirce, who offered a valuable bit of writing advice during an unrelated personal appointment. Her books have been a constant in my life since I first received 'The Intuitive Way' many years ago as a gift from my friend Karen Klein. Soon after, 'Frequency' became one of my 'Bibles.'

I hadn't planned to write a book. However, one day I had a strong intuitive nudge to share some of my life experiences in writing. The intention was to offer hope and to demonstrate how we are all able to live with inner peace and unlimited possibilities. So I began to write. Shortly after, I reached out to an amazingly talented woman, Kris M. Smith. She edited a few pages for me and from that I gained some new knowledge about how to write.

After writing out a number of my experiences, I loosely arranged them into book form. When I wondered where to go from there, I was soon drawn to contact my long-time friend Joan Kaminski. She has always been a source of loving support and encouragement. Joan did major structural and substantive editing which was of enormous help to me. It helped me rearrange and organize the stories, creating a better flow to the book overall.

After more writing and rewriting, another treasured friend and gifted healer, Paula Kelly edited and then re-edited along the way. She encouraged me to be more descriptive. Since these are all lived experiences that are a natural part of me, I hadn't realized all of the details I took for granted and left out. Paula questioned and prodded and got me to see what a reader would want to know beyond what I had written. She also lifted me up with her loving, encouraging words when I got bogged down or when I had to put it all aside for over a year as I cared for my mother in her last year of life here. Paula has been a continuous beacon of light in my life.

Very early on, a fellow RN, traveler, adventurer and dear friend, Karen Frazier Brown, edited for typos and also offered useful input from a reader's perspective. She patiently, and with good humor, took my numerous calls while trying to create a subtitle. We laughed at the craziness of it all. Karen and I met while working in a remote bush hospital in rural Alaska and have remained close friends.

Although completely mystified over how I do what I do, my brother Marty Saulenas, a gifted thriller/mystery writer read the manuscript. He offered input on the title, and wrote the draft for the back cover.

So many other friends offered encouragement and support along the way as well. They know my life's work and encouraged me to share it through my writing.

My beautiful mother, Rose Saulenas, who remained youthful, spry, and social until months before she died, was my biggest fan.

Knowing and accepting when it was her time to pass on, she hopped into bed one evening, bid my brothers, her puppy and myself a loving, joyful, goodbye. She then closed her eyes, fell asleep, and quietly passed on, just shy of her 96th birthday.

Besides being only a phone call away, my good friend Margie Zable Fisher found Booklocker for me.

Without Angela and her team at Booklocker, I'm not sure I would have gotten this published. Angela makes it as easy as possible to get through the publishing process. She also seems to genuinely care about supporting authors and their art form.

I am grateful for all that Angela has created, and all that she and her team do.

My heartfelt thanks to everyone along the way for all of the love, wonderful experiences, and time shared in this amazing life together.

About the Author

As an Intuitive, and former RN, Sharon Saulenas has offered hope, healing, insight, and inner peace to many, including those at end of life. She believes we all have the ability to 'connect' and reach past the physical plane to a place of Divine guidance, joy, and inner peace. A native New Englander, she has lived as far north as the arctic circle and as far south as Ecuador.

Currently she assists others in connecting with the Divine Wisdom and developing their fullness. She also helps those with end-of-life concerns release fear and find inner peace.

As an adolescent she was once asked how she could be so comfortable approaching and talking with strangers. She replied by saying" I never consider them strangers, only friends I haven't met yet."